Art of
Indian
Cuisine

To my Dad
for all that I am . . .

ISBN: 18-5605-537-X

Published by
Silverdale Books
An imprint of
Bookmart Ltd
Registered Number 2372865
Trading as Bookmart Limited
Desford Road, Enderby
Leicester, LE9 5AD

© ROLI BOOKS PVT. LTD., 1999
LUSTRE PRESS PVT. LTD.

Text: ROCKY MOHAN

Photographs: DHEERAJ PAUL

Food Styling: PRAMOD KAPOOR

Conceived and designed at
Roli CAD Centre

Printed and bound by
APP Printing, Singapore

ROCKY MOHAN

Art of
Indian
Cuisine

Photographs   Dheeraj Paul

Food Styling   Pramod Kapoor

Silverdale Books

C O N T E N T S

5

PREFACE

It all started for me when my two sisters and I were young, school-going children in Lucknow, which, I believe, has long been acknowledged as the capital of both culture and tasteful cuisine in India. My parents had shifted to Lucknow from Solan, near Shimla, the then summer capital of India. My father, Padma Bhushan Col. Ved Rattan Mohan, who was a Member of Parliament (Rajya Sabha) and the Chairman and Managing Director of Mohan Meakin Ltd., was a connoisseur of speciality cooking. My mother, Comilla Mohan, was one of the most gracious hostesses I have ever come across. It is from them that I inherited a palate for gourmet cooking.

When my older sister got married, chefs were especially flown in to cook Kashmiri, Punjabi, Avadhi and Rampuri food. I spent the four days it took to prepare the delicacies with the chefs, questioning them keenly about each procedure and why it had to be followed in a particular way. This interest spilt over into our home kitchen, when I spent time with our family cooks giving them suggestions and occasionally forcing them to follow them. They would reluctantly agree, and, at times, the outcome was impressive. Encouraged, I started cooking at least one dish every week. This enforced effort turned into enjoyment as I became more and more proficient. Thereafter, there was no looking back. I started cooking food regularly, either following recipes of experienced cooks or experimenting with cookery books. That is how I got involved in the rich history, variety and tradition of Indian cuisine. Over the years, my travels have taken me from Kashmir to Tamil Nadu, West Bengal to the Rann of Kutch . . . Apart from being exposed to the wealth of traditional cuisine, I have also came across cuisines which have not been documented till date. This has led me to explore the techniques of cooking by chefs who have inherited the art of cooking good food from their forefathers.

In this book I have tried, not only to create new recipes, but also adapt some to suit the gadgets of a modern kitchen and a busy lifestyle. This has made them 'easy to make'!

My wife, Rekha, has been the 'guinea pig' of my experimentation with cooking. I cannot thank her enough for her never-ending support, encouragement and constructive criticism. Thanks also to my sons, Siddharth Rattan and Vijay Rattan, who have from a very young age, been requesting me to cook from my collection of recipes.

I would like to place on record my personal appreciation to my cooks, Hari Kishan Sharma and Munshi Ram who have helped me over the years to document these recipes and cook them for my family and friends.

I would also like to thank Bubli Seth for presenting me with my first cook book and, I guess, starting me off in the right direction. Further, my heartfelt appreciation goes out to Loveleena Shah, Naushaba Siddique, Pareen Khan, Munna Mian, Haji Rahim, Anisha Kohli, Ahad Waza, Dr. Pathak, Mehr Bhargava, Zohre Ansari and Raju.

A special word about Chootu, my man Friday: his contribution during the final photography shoot cannot but be emphasised. He was there whenever needed—helping Pramod Kapoor, the food stylist, and Dheeraj Paul, the extremely talented photographer, preparing for the shoot, getting the accessories, organising the studio, and last but not the least, cleaning up after the day's work.

On the last day of the shoot he told us that he wanted to organise a dinner for all of us where he would put the ideas he had imbibed during this period to use. We agreed to meet just after the Id festival. Unfortunately, it was not to be. I lost Chootu on the night of Id when he had an accident on his way home. I shall miss him immensely, and I pray for his departed soul.

This book could not have been produced without the invaluable help of Mrs. Kavita Bhartiya of Ogaan, Mrs. Rekha Mohan, Mrs. Kiran Kapoor, Karmos and Sachin who assisted Dheeraj Paul. Mr. Pramod Kapoor and Dheeraj Paul have given the book its shape with their food styling and photography, respectively. We enjoyed great team spirit and derived much pleasure in putting the book together.

My recommendation to the reader is that when you start using this cook book, make it a habit to put down your comments on each recipe that you try. Do also make a note of what others have to say about the food. This will help you remember which recipe you have been able to cook well, and has been a success with your family, friends and guests. It is a good practice to remember the occasion for which you cooked the recipe.

Make this book a personal one. Instead of being a mere collection of recipes, it will not only provide you with the pleasure of cooking, but will evoke memories of memorable meals cooked for your family and friends. I sincerely hope you enjoy using this book as much as I have enjoyed writing it.

INDIAN SPICES AND INGREDIENTS

Spices are the very heart and soul of Indian cuisine. They form the foundation of a cuisine that has existed for centuries. It is virtually impossible to cook Indian dishes without spices, even if they are only red chillies and salt.

Each and every spice has its own function and should be used to develop the flavour as required. The attributes of the various spices are varied and they must be used in the proportions recommended. You may decide to vary these proportions, but a word of caution is required here. Do not vary the quantity until you have read this chapter fully and understood the significance and purpose of these spices.

Garlic: This is used either coarsely or finely chopped, cracked, whole or ground with a little water. Garlic, being a strong spice, has a very distinct flavour and must be used cautiously. It complements ginger when used with it in a dish.

Ginger: A root, this must be used after scraping the skin with either a sharp knife or a potato peeler. To ensure that it is fresh, make sure that the root you use is firm to the touch and not wrinkled. Cut the ginger coarsely when you require to have a distinct flavour. Ginger can also be ground with a little water, or only the juice of the root most may be used. Ginger complements garlic in most Indian dishes. It also helps in reducing the pungency of the flavour of garlic. Dry ginger powder is made by drying the root and then grinding it until it

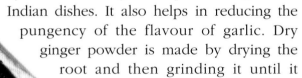

1   Mace (*javitri*)
2   Cloves (*laung*)
3   Black cumin
    (*kala jeera*)
    seeds
4   Cumin seed
    (*jeera*) powder
5   Black pepper
    (*kala mirch*)
6   Cumin (*jeera*)
    seeds
7   Garam masala

is in powder form. Dry ginger powder is used extensively in Kashmiri dishes.

Onions: Onions play a fundamental role in almost all Indian dishes. Onions can be used in different ways, most commonly being sliced or chopped. Onions are also ground with a little water or fried, and used either in the beginning or later, as the recipe proceeds. Onions can taste different, depending on the way they are used. If used quartered, as a vegetable, they impart their own flavour and taste. When fried, they impart a nutty sweet taste, and when ground, they form the base of a thick sauce or gravy.

Asafoetida: This resinous gum has a very strong and unpleasant smell. It must only be used in very small quantities. The best way to control the quantity that you have to use, is to keep the resin in a glass jar and add water. Use the water as indicated in the recipe.

Cardamoms: One of the world's most expensive spices, grown mainly in India and Sri Lanka, there are two varieties—the large, black-brown ones, which have a heavier flavour and the small green ones which are aromatic and have a delicate flavour. The flavour is best if only the seeds are used to make a powder.

Chilli and chilli powder: There are at least 20 known varieties of chilli powders. The range of chillies can be from white and yellow to saffron and red in colour. While capsicums or peppers are mild and flavoured, Goan chillies are dark red in colour and not pungent. Green chillies are similar to fresh red chillies and their seeds are the most

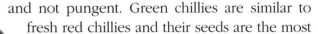

1 Aniseed *(saunf)*
2 Anise pepper
3 Coriander seed *(dhaniya)*
4 Mustard *(rai)* seeds
5 Yellow mustard
6 Star anise *(chakri phool)*
7 Coriander seed *(dhaniya)* powder
8 Black mustard *(sarson)* seeds
9 Fennel seeds *(moti saunf)*

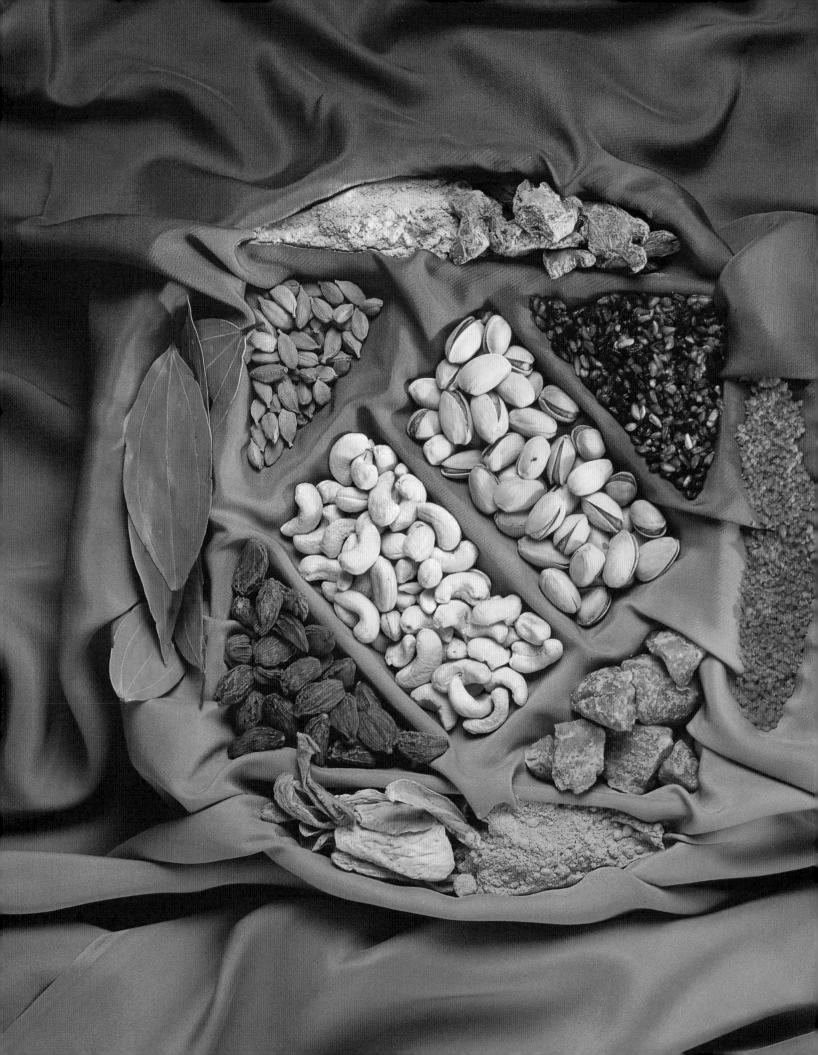

pungent. Red Kashmiri chillies are very mild and can be used for colouring. Red chillies, either whole or finely chopped or sliced, are used for flavouring.

Cinnamon: Most Indian food is cooked with cassia bark, which is a good substitute for real cinnamon. However, it does not have the delicate flavour of cinnamon as its flavour is much stronger.

Cloves: Cloves are the dried flower buds of an evergreen plant. The oil of cloves contains phenol, which is a good antiseptic and helps in preserving food.

Coriander: Coriander seed powder is a very important spice in Indian food. Fresh coriander leaves are used for garnishing. Coriander has a strong, pungent smell but is almost indispensable to Indian cuisine.

Cumin seeds: Cumin seeds come in two varieties: white and black. The white variety is the more common one and is used as extensively as coriander seed powder, while the black variety is more aromatic and peppery.

Curry leaves : These impart a subtle flavour when fried until they are crisp. They are popular in South Indian dishes.

Fennel seeds: Fennel seeds are a common ingredient for flavouring stocks and sauces. They are used as a pickling spice and for flavouring curries. Used extensively as an ingredient in *paan* and as an effective digestive, they freshen and sweeten the breath.

14

1   Turmeric *(haldi)* powder / Turmeric *(haldi)* whole
2   Coconut *(nariyal)*
3   Sesame seeds *(til)*
4   Carom seeds *(ajwain)*
5   Fenugreek seeds *(methi dana)* / Dry fenugreek leaves *(kasoori methi)*
6   Charoli seeds *(chironji)*
7   Almonds *(badam)*
8   Poppy seeds *(khus khus)*
9   Nigella seeds *(kalongi)*
10 Red chilli powder *(lal mirch)* / Red chillies *(lal mirch)*

Fenugreek: Fenugreek seeds and leaves are used differently. The seeds are square, flat and yellowish-brown in colour. Care must be taken in using the seeds as they are bitter and the quantity used must be controlled. The leaves are even more bitter and the taste imparts a unique flavour to the dish.

Mace: Mace is a part of the nutmeg. It is the shell of the nutmeg kernel. It has a flavour similar to nutmeg but is more delicate and is used in rice dishes.

Mustard oil: A pungent, deep yellow oil extracted from mustard seeds, mustard oil must be used after raising its temperature to a smoking point and then cooling it before any ingredients are added.

Nutmeg: This is used to make fragrant garam masala. The kernel must be finely grated just before use. Excessive use must be avoided as it can be poisonous.

Poppy seeds: White poppy seeds, roasted and ground, are used to provide a nutty flavour and to thicken gravies.

Saffron: The world's most expensive spice, saffron must be soaked in either warm milk or water and used at the end of cooking a dish. To preserve the flavour, grind 10 gm of saffron with 8 sugar cubes.

Turmeric: Turmeric is a rhizome of the ginger family and is orange-yellow in colour.

1 Ginger powder *(sonth)* / Dry ginger *(adrak)*
2 Bayleaves *(tejpatta)*
3 Green cardamoms *(elaichi)*
4 Pomegranate seeds *(anardana)*
5 Asafoetida *(hing)*
6 Pistachios *(pista)*
7 Cashewnut *(kaju)*
8 Brown cardamoms *(bari elaichi)*
9 Jaggery *(gur)*
10 Dry mango / Dry mango powder *(amchur)*

15

MAKING MASALAS AT HOME

Making masalas at home is an essential part of the Indian cuisine. Here are some recipes you will find very useful.

Standard garam masala

18 gm / 4 tbsp	Black cumin seeds *(kala jeera)*
18 gm / 4 tbsp	Cumin seeds *(jeera)*
40 / 4 tbsp	Cloves *(laung)*
12	Bayleaves *(tej patta)*
40 / 4 tbsp	Black cardamom *(bari elaichi)* seeds
40 / 4 tbsp	Green cardamom *(elaichi)* seeds
6	Cinnamon *(dalchini)* sticks, 1" long
25 / 2 tbsp	Peppercorns *(kali mirch)*
1 gm / ½ tsp	Mace *(javitri)*, powdered
9 gm / 2 tbsp	Dry ginger powder *(sonth)*

Method: Dry roast the black cumin seeds, cumin seeds, cloves, bayleaves, black cardamom seeds, green cardamom seeds, cinnamon sticks and peppercorns on low heat until aromatic. Remove from heat and cool. Put all the roasted spices, mace and dry ginger powder in an electric blender and grind to a fine powder. Then pass the powder through a fine sieve. Store in an airtight container.

Fragrant garam masala

6	Cinnamon *(dalchini)* sticks, 1" long
3 gm / 2 tsp	Cardamom *(elaichi)* seeds
3 gm / 1 tsp	Cloves *(laung)*
2 gm / 1 tsp	Mace *(javitri)*, powdered
1 gm / ½	Nutmeg *(jaiphal)*, grated

Method: Dry roast the cinnamon sticks, cardamom seeds, cloves and mace powder on low heat until aromatic. Mix the dry, roasted spices with the grated nutmeg and blend to make a fine powder. Then follow the same method as mentioned for the Standard Garam Masala.

Kashmiri garam masala

10 gm / 4 tsp	Green cardamom *(elaichi)* seeds
3 gm / 2 tsp	Black cumin *(kala jeera)* seeds
12 gm / 2 tsp	Peppercorns *(kali mirch)*
6	Cinnamon *(dalchini)* sticks, 1" long
3 gm / 1 tsp	Cloves *(laung)*
1 gm / ½	Nutmeg *(jaiphal)*, grated

Method: Use the same method as for the Standard and Fragrant garam masalas.

Tandoori garam masala

3 gm / 2 tsp	Turmeric *(haldi)* powder
1½ gm / 1 tsp	Red chilli *(lal mirch)* powder
2 gm / 1 tsp	Garam Masala (see above)
2 gm / ½ tsp	Garlic *(lasan)* powder
1 gm / ½ tsp	Dry ginger powder *(sonth)*
1 tsp	Cinnamon *(dalchini)*, ground

Method: Mix all the above ingredients thoroughly, and store in an airtight container for later use.

Hara masala

This paste is made from spices and fresh greens. When added to any vegetarian preparation, it imparts extra flavour, enhancing the taste.

12 gm / 3 tsp	Garlic *(lasan),* chopped
32 gm / 4 tsp	Ginger *(adrak),* scraped and chopped
15 gm / 1 cup	Mint *(pudina)* leaves, finely chopped
25 gm / 1 cup	Coriander leaves *(hara dhaniya),* finely chopped
100 ml / ½ cup	White vinegar *(sirka)*
	Salt to taste
4 gm / 2 tsp	Fragrant garam masala (see p. 18)
3 gm / 2 tsp	Turmeric *(haldi)* powder
150 ml / ¾ cup	Vegetable oil

Method: Put the garlic, ginger, mint leaves, coriander leaves and vinegar in an electric blender and blend until the mixture is smooth. Mix salt and ground spices. Heat oil and add the blended mixture. Bring to a boil, then turn off the heat. Cool and bottle in an airtight container. If the oil does not cover the top of the masala, then heat some more oil and add to it.

19

Madras curry powder

Curry powder as such does not exist in India—each dish is flavoured with its own unique blend of spices, which are normally mixed and ground just before use. This masala was developed by the British during the Raj. This recipe is one of the oldest and is claimed to be the authentic one. Use this masala in meats as a substitute for other spices, and for tempering vegetarian dishes. Make enough and store in an airtight container for use later.

To make 500 gm:

80 gm / 13 tbsp	Coriander seeds *(dhaniya)*
60 gm / 15 tbsp	Turmeric *(haldi)* powder
13 gm / 1 ½ tbsp	Fenugreek seeds *(methi dana)*
60 gm / 10 tbsp	Dry ginger powder *(sonth)*
75 gm / ¾ cup	Peppercorns *(kali mirch)*
60 gm / 120	Red chillies *(lal mirch),* dry
40 gm / 265	Green cardamoms *(elaichi)*
40 gm / 80	Cinnamon *(dalchini)* sticks, 2" each

Method: Roast the coriander seeds on low heat until aromatic and the colour changes. Cool and blend with all the other ingredients and grind to a fine powder.

FLAVOURING AND SMOKING TECHNIQUES

Classical Indian cuisine has some processes which are very similar to other classical cuisines, the art of smoking and flavouring meat or mince being the most practised.

Baghar: Aromatic spices play a very important role in Indian cooking. These spices are cloves, cumin seeds, cardamom seeds and pods and cinnamon sticks, just to name a few. When these spices are added to a heated cooking medium, they release their flavours into the cooking medium. This process of flavouring is called *baghar*. One can also experiment doing *baghar* with dry red and green chillies and garlic cloves.

Method: Heat the cooking medium until it is almost smoking; reduce the heat to medium and add the spices or condiments. Wait till the spices or condiments change colour and float upon the oil, then remove the pan from the heat. This highly flavoured cooking medium can be added at either the beginning or at the end of cooking (according to the recipe).

Dhungar: This is a technique of smoking uncooked meats or a cooked dish. The spices or condiments used are similar to those used for *baghar. Dhungar* can be done by any of the three methods:

Method 1: Put a live piece of charcoal in a *katori* (small metal bowl). Blow the ashes from it and pour a little refined oil or butter on it. When the oil starts to smoke, put the *katori* in the centre of the meat or cooked food and cover the pan tightly to trap the flavoured smoke. Leave the pan covered for at least 20 minutes.

Method 2: Put a piece of live coal in a *katori* and put the recommended spice over it. Pour some cooking medium over the spice and when it smokes, put the *katori* in the pan and cover immediately. Leave the pan covered for at least 30 minutes.

Method 3: This method is used mainly for uncooked meats. Instead of using a *katori* as in the earlier methods, the use of a large onion peel is suggested. Place the live piece of coal on the onion peel and put the spices on it. When it starts smoking, put the peel in the centre of the meat and cover immediately to trap the smoke.

Dum: *Dum* means to mature a cooked dish. The *dum* technique is usually applied to Mughlai recipes.

Method: After the completion of cooking, the pan is sealed either with dough or by putting a weight on the cover of the pan. The pan is then put on a very slow fire or in a cooling oven for at least 30 minutes. This process enhances the flavours as the ingredients are steamed and are allowed to blend thoroughly.

Bhunao: This technique implies cooking ground masalas on high heat by adding small quantities of liquid just when the masala has little or no moisture left. This process of adding liquid is used to lower the temperature of the cooking masala to save it from burning and also to allow the spices to have a toasted flavour.

Method: Add the liquid (water or yoghurt) to the masala and scrape the bottom of the pan. Repeat the process at least three times or as recommended in the recipe.

Note: When you *bhunao*, do not let your attention be diverted. You may burn the spices if constant attention is not paid to the process.

Durust karna: In the case of almost all Avadhi dishes, the cooking medium must be flavoured prior to its use.

Method: Heat at least 2 cups of refined oil in a pan with a lid to a smoking point and then reduce the heat to low. Sprinkle 1 ½ tbsp of *kewra* water or *gulab jal* into the cooking medium, and instantly cover the pan with the lid to avoid any splutter. When the crackle stops, add 6-7 green cardamoms and fry until they change colour. Remove the cardamoms from the cooking medium and discard. Remove the pan from the heat and keep the cooking medium for use later.

TRADITIONAL COOKING STYLES AND BASIC INDIAN RECIPES

Indian cuisine follows several age-old methods of cooking which are reflected in the names of the recipes themselves. There are also some basic recipes which form an inherent part of the main recipe.

TRADITIONAL PREPARATIONS

Kalia / Qalia
Kalia is a curry which is either water, yoghurt or milk-based. The gravy of the finished dish is light.

Korma / Qurma
Korma is a curry which is *ghee,* butter or oil-based and where most of the water added while cooking evaporates and the cooking medium floats to the surface.

Do-piyaza
Any meat preparation which is cooked with vegetables is called *Do-piyaza.* It does not, as is commonly believed, refer to any meat dish cooked with a large quantity of onions, or the fact that onions are added twice, as the name suggests. However, difference of opinion on this subject has yet to be resolved.

Salan
A meat preparation that is cooked with vegetables. (This is true for preparations which can trace their origin to Lucknow, Avadh and Kashmir. The Kashmiri pundits / brahmins cook meat with milk and not yoghurt; this is also called a *salan).* Pure vegetarian dishes prepared with a gravy are also referred to as *salan.*

Mussallam
Any meat (chicken, goat or lamb, leg of meat, vegetable (cauli- fish ...) or flower, bitter gourd ...) that is cooked whole is called *mussallam.*

Kebab
Kebabs are chunks of meat, fish or chicken, grilled (broiled) on skewers over an open flame or in a tandoor (clay oven). Kebabs probably originated in

the Caucasus where the mountain people speared meat pieces and then cooked them over an open fire.

Biryani

Meat cooked with fragrant spices, combined with rice in layers and finished with *dum* is known as *biryani*. Its origins can be traced to Moghul Delhi and Hyderabad, where originally, the leftover cooked meat was used in combination with rice to make a complete meal.

Pulao

Rice, when cooked in meat and / or vegetable stock, is called a *pulao*.

Teheri

Rice cooked with turmeric pow-der and a com-bination of vege-tables or meat, is called *teheri*. Saffron is also used to put a finishing touch to the dish.

Yakhni

Yakhni is stock made of meat, vegetables and spices and is used for cooking rice. In Kashmir there is a meat preparation made with yoghurt and dry ginger powder, which is also called *yakhni*.

BASIC INDIAN RECIPES

Clarified butter *(ghee)*

If you are living in the United States, United Kingdom, Australia, New Zealand or Canada, you will find *ghee* in any Indian grocery store. If not, you can very easily make it at home with a little effort.

Method: Heat some unsalted butter until it melts and froths. Remove the foam that rises from the top and once clear, pour the melted butter into a heat-proof container. Discard the milk solids that are left behind. Leave to cool at room temperature and then chill. When the chilled fat rises to the top, spoon it off, leaving the *ghee* behind. If you would like to refine the *ghee* further, then heat the *ghee* and strain it through a muslin cloth.

Note. In India, cooking oils with distinctive flavours are used, depending on the region. In eastern India, mustard oil and coconut oil are very popular, while in the south, *til* or sesame seed oil and coconut oil are

used. It is recommended that a tasteless refined oil be used. Refined peanut oil is also suitable.

Cottage cheese (paneer)

Paneer is Indian cottage cheese / cream cheese. Like *ghee* it is quite easily available. If not, you can make it in your kitchen.

Method: Pour full-fat milk into a saucepan and bring to a boil. Stir so that no skin forms on top. As the milk reaches a full boil, add lemon juice. The proportion is 1 ½ tbsp lemon juice : 3 cups of milk. Remove from heat and wait until firm curds are formed. Strain through a muslin cloth. Tie the ends of the cloth and hang for at least 45 minutes. Remove. To remove the moisture further put a weight on top. Leave for at least a couple of hours to drain. Remove from the cloth and cut the paneer into cubes.

Tomato purée

Tomato pulp blended to a smooth cream.

Method: Peel, deseed and chop the tomatoes. Transfer to a pan. Add 1 lt of water, 8 cloves, 8 green cardamoms, 15 gm ginger, 10 gm garlic, 5 bayleaves and 5 peppercorns and cook on medium heat till the tomatoes are tender. Cool and process to a pulp.

Wholemilk fudge (khoya)

This is Indian-style condensed milk.

Method: Bring full-cream milk to a quick boil in a heavy-bottomed pan. Cook until almost all the moisture evaporates and the milk solids are left behind to form a very granular and lumpy dough. The larger the pan, the quicker it will be made. Stirring constantly is very important. Approximate conversion: 4 cups full-cream milk will yield approximately 100 gm of *khoya*.

Coconut milk (nariyal ka doodh)

Coconut milk must not be mistaken for the clear liquid in the green nut. The clear liquid is good for drinking. Coconut milk is entirely different. It is used for enriching dishes because it is very rich in fat. Always reduce the heat before adding coconut milk to a dish and never boil while the cooking pan is covered, as the milk curdles easily.

Method: Grate fresh, mature coconut. Add measured quantities of hot water (as per recipe) and extract the milk. The first extract is called 'thick coconut milk'. Similarly, the second extract is called 'thin co-conut milk'. Fresh coconut milk may be substi-tuted with the packaged variety.

Yoghurt (dahi)

Unflavoured yog-hurt or *dahi,* as it is called in India, is used very extensively in the cooking of Indian

24

dishes. Use a slightly sour flavour. The German natural yoghurt comes the closest.

Method: Boil milk and keep it aside till it becomes lukewarm. Add 2 tsp yoghurt to the milk and mix well. Allow it to ferment for 6-8 hours.

Gram flour *(besan)*

Besan is used in certain dishes, snacks and in the making of Indian breads. *Besan* has a very distinctive flavour and must not be substituted with any other flour.

Method: Roast yellow split peas in a pan, stirring constantly, so that they do not burn. Remove the pan from the heat and cool. Then blend the roasted peas at a high speed or pound with a mortar and pestle. Sieve, and keep in an airtight container.

Garlic and Ginger pastes

Garlic and ginger pastes are used extensively in most of the recipes.

Method: Make the individual pastes separately in large quantities by mixing in an electric blender with a small quantity of water. Blend at a high speed to make a smooth paste. Remove and store in airtight containers and keep in the refrigerator for use later. The pastes will keep for upto five to six weeks.

Rice

Rice in India is an indispensable part of most meals. This is even truer for the coastal areas. In the north and central part of the subcontinent, though breads are eaten, rice forms a major part of the diet. India is known to cultivate many qualities of rice and the king of all varieties of *rice* is the long-grain Basmati variety.

Rice / Water ratio

For short or medium-grain variety of rice:

    1 cup rice : 1½ cups of water
    2 cups rice : 2½ cups of water
    3 cups rice : 3½ cups of water

    Long-grain rice absorbs a much greater quantity of water than the short or medium-grain variety.

    1 cup rice : 2 cups of water
    2 cups rice : 3½ cups of water
    3 cups rice : 5 cups of water

Note. Soaking rice in plenty of water prior to cooking, improves the yield and also provides for longer and separate grains. Frying the rice prior to adding the water also keeps the grains separate after cooking.

SINDHI MURGH

(Succulent chicken legs)

Serves: 4

INGREDIENTS

8	Chicken drumsticks
150 ml / ¾ cup	Yoghurt *(dahi)*, whisked
1 ½ gm / 1 tsp	Turmeric *(haldi)* powder
2 gm / 1 ½ tsp	Red chilli *(lal mirch)* powder
2 gm / 1 tsp	Garam masala (standard, see p. 18)
	Salt to taste
100 ml / ½ cup	Clarified butter *(ghee)* / refined oil
6	Cloves *(laung)*
6	Peppercorns *(kali mirch)*, whole
2 gm / 1 tsp	Poppy seeds *(khus khus)*
2 gm / 1 tsp	Coriander seeds *(dhaniya)*
1 gm / ½ tsp	Cumin seeds *(jeera)*
4	Onions *(piyaz)*, medium, chopped
2	Tomatoes *(tamatar)*, medium, chopped
12 gm / 3 tbsp	Mint *(pudina)* leaves
1	Ginger *(adrak)*, 1 ½" piece, chopped
8	Garlic *(lasan)* cloves, chopped

METHOD

◆ Marinate the chicken pieces in the yoghurt, turmeric, red chilli powder, garam masala and salt for 1 hour.

◆ Heat 2 tablespoons of clarified butter / oil in a pan; add the cloves, peppercorns, poppy seeds, coriander seeds and cumin seeds. Fry until they crackle; add the onions and sauté until the onions are browned. Remove the pan from the heat and cool. Put the contents of the pan into a blender and make a paste with the tomatoes, mint leaves, ginger and garlic. Blend until the mixture is smooth.

◆ Heat the remaining clarified butter / oil; add the chicken pieces with the marinade. Cook until the water has evaporated. Cook until the chicken turns a light brown.

◆ Add the onion paste and 1 cup of hot water. Bring to a boil. Cover the pan and simmer, stirring occasionally until tender.

Sindhi Murgh ▶

ADRAKI MURGH

(Ginger chicken in rich tomato gravy)

Serves: 4

INGREDIENTS

600 to 700 gm	Chicken, without skin, cut into 8 pieces
3 gm / 2 tsp	Cumin seeds *(jeera)*
	Salt to taste

For the marinade:

12 gm / 2 tsp	Ginger *(adrak)* paste
6 gm / 1 tsp	Garlic *(lasan)* paste
1 ½ gm / 1 tsp	Coriander *(dhaniya)* powder
3 gm / 1 tsp	Cumin seed *(jeera)* powder
1 ½ gm / 1 tsp	Red chilli *(lal mirch)* powder
3	Green cardamom *(elaichi)*, powdered
100 ml / ½ cup	Malt vinegar *(sirka)*
300 ml / 1 ½ cup	Yoghurt *(dahi)*, whisked
100 ml / ½ cup	Clarified butter *(ghee)* / refined oil
1 ½ cups	Tomatoes *(tamatar)*, blanched, peeled and chopped
7 ½ ml / 1 ½ tsp	Red edible colour

METHOD

◆ Add the chicken pieces to the marinade. Mix well and keep aside for 2 hours.

◆ Heat the clarified butter / oil; add the cumin seeds until they crackle. Add the chicken with the marinade and stir. Put in the tomatoes and salt and cook on medium heat until the chicken becomes tender and the gravy, thick.

◆ Add the red edible colour and mix well.

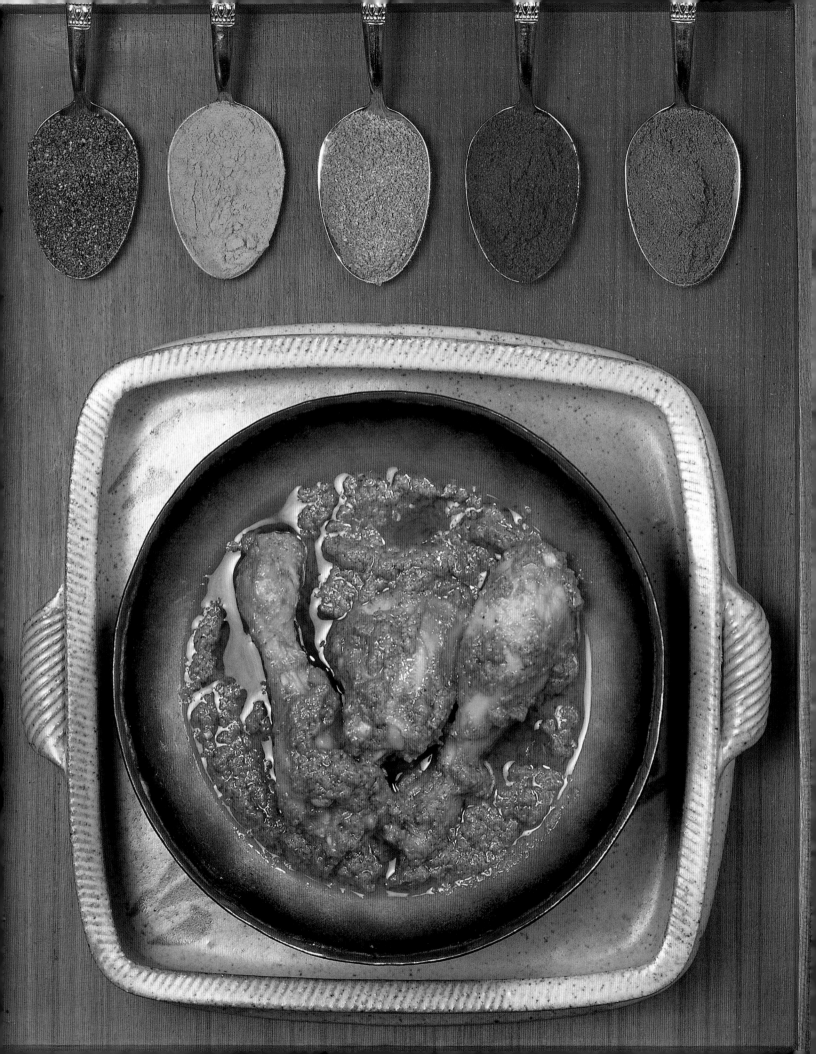

MURGH KASOORI METHI

(Delectable chicken with aromatic dried fenugreek leaves)

Serves: 4-6

INGREDIENTS

700 gm	Chicken, without skin, 8 pieces
100 ml / ½ cup	Clarified butter *(ghee)* / refined oil
3	Cloves *(laung)*
2	Black cardamoms *(bari elaichi)*, cracked
3	Onions *(piyaz)*, medium-sized, sliced
12 gm / 3 tsp	Garlic *(lasan)*, chopped
25 gm / 3 tsp	Ginger *(adrak)*, chopped
18 gm / 6	Green chillies *(hari mirch)*, without the stems
600 ml / 3 cups	Water
3 gm / 2 tbsp	Dried fenugreek leaves *(kasoori methi)*
100 ml / ½ cup	Yoghurt *(dahi)*
1 ½ gm / 1 tsp	Red chilli *(lal mirch)* powder
1 gm / ½ tsp	Turmeric *(haldi)* powder
	Salt to taste

METHOD

◆ Heat the clarified butter / oil in a heavy-bottomed vessel. Add the cloves and the black cardamoms. Fry until they crackle. Add the onions, stir for a minute; add the garlic, ginger and the green chillies and stir for 30 seconds, so that they are just about sealed by the oil. Add one cup of hot water and bring to a boil. Let the water evaporate and add the dried fenugreek leaves. Add half a cup of hot water and let it evaporate again. Thereafter, sauté until all the ingredients turn golden in colour.
◆ Add the chicken, yoghurt, red chilli powder, turmeric and salt and stir. Cook until the yoghurt is absorbed; then add 1½ cups water and cook until the chicken becomes tender and the clarified butter / oil comes to the surface.

Murgh Kasoori Methi ▶

MURGH DHANIYA

(Slow-cooked coriander chicken)

Serves: 4

INGREDIENTS

700 gm	Chicken, without skin, 8 pieces
100 ml / 1 cup	Yoghurt *(dahi)*, whisked
	Salt to taste
100 ml / ½ cup	Clarified butter *(ghee)* / refined oil
5	Green cardamoms *(elaichi)*
10	Cloves *(laung)*
1	Cinnamon *(dalchini)* stick, 1"
180 gm / 1½ cup	Onions *(piyaz)*, thinly sliced
16 gm / 4 tsp	Garlic *(lasan)*, chopped
30 gm / 4 tsp	Ginger *(adrak)*, chopped
18 gm / 6	Green chillies *(hari mirch)*, finely sliced
1 ½ gm / 1 tsp	Red chilli *(lal mirch)* powder
1 cup	Tomatoes *(tamatar)*, chopped
40 gm / 1½ cups	Coriander leaves *(hara dhaniya)*, chopped
30 gm / 4 tsp	Ginger *(adrak)*, juliennes, *(long, thin strips)*

METHOD

◆ Marinate the chicken pieces in the yoghurt and salt for 1 hour.
◆ Heat the clarified butter / oil in a pan; add the cardamoms, cloves and cinnamon. Fry until they crackle. Add the sliced onions and sauté until golden brown. Add the chopped garlic, ginger and sliced green chillies. Cook and stir until the water evaporates. Add the red chilli powder and tomatoes. Cook until the masala is well blended and the clarified butter / oil comes to the surface.
◆ Add the marinated chicken pieces. Stir until the yoghurt is absorbed. Add 1 cup of water and bring to a boil. Simmer until the chicken is tender.
◆ Sprinkle the coriander leaves and ginger juliennes and seal the pan tightly. Put on *dum* (see p. 21) for 10 minutes.

MURGH PUDINA

(Chicken à la mint)

Serves: 4

INGREDIENTS

600 to 700 gm	Chicken, without skin, cut into 8 pieces
12 gm / 2 tsp	Ginger *(adrak)* paste
12 gm / 2 tsp	Garlic *(lasan)* paste
200 ml / 1 cup	Clarified butter *(ghee)* / refined oil
	Salt to taste
200 ml / 1 cup	Yoghurt *(dahi)*
200 ml / 1 cup	Wholemilk fudge *(khoya)*, liquidised
60 gm / 20	Green chillies *(hari mirch)*, pricked with a toothpick or fork
25 gm / 1½ cups	Mint leaves *(pudina)*, chopped
400 ml / 2 cups	Coconut milk *(nariyal ka doodh)*
48 gm / 60	Almonds *(badam)*, blanched, peeled, sliced, fried until light brown, drained and kept aside
48 gm / 90	Sultanas *(kishmish)*, soaked in water, sliced, fried for 2 minutes, drained and kept aside

METHOD

◆ Marinate the chicken pieces in the ginger and garlic pastes for 45 minutes.

◆ Heat the clarified butter / oil; add the chicken pieces with the marinade and fry until lightly browned. Add the salt, yoghurt and wholemilk fudge. Stir until the yoghurt dries up. Add the green chillies and mint leaves and stir. Put in the coconut milk and cook on low heat until the meat becomes tender and has a thick gravy. Add the fried almonds and sultanas and stir.

Murgh Pudina ▶

MURGH KAJU

(Hot chicken delight flavoured with cashewnuts)

Serves: 4

INGREDIENTS

700 to 750 gm	Chicken, without skin, 8 pieces
½	Coconut *(nariyal)*, grated
12	Garlic *(lasan)*, cloves
16 gm / 2 tsp	Ginger *(adrak)*, chopped
15 gm / 2½ tbsp	Coriander seeds *(dhaniya)*
3 gm / 1 ½ tsp	Cumin seeds *(jeera)*
3 gm / 6	Red chillies *(lal mirch)*, dry
6	Cloves *(laung)*
3	Cinnamon *(dalchini)* sticks, 1"
1 cup	Cashewnuts *(kaju)*
180 gm / ¾ cup	Onions *(piyaz)*, chopped
2 gm / 1 tsp	Peppercorn *(kali mirch)*, coarsely powdered
100 ml / ½ cup	Clarified butter *(ghee)* / refined oil

METHOD

◆ Roast the coconut, garlic, ginger, coriander seeds, cumin seeds, whole red chillies, cloves and cinnamon over low heat until aromatic. Add ½ a cup of cashewnuts and onions and roast all together for 10 minutes, stirring all the time. Turn off the heat and cool. Add the peppercorn powder and grind all together.

◆ Separately grind another ¼ cup of cashewnuts with a little water.

◆ Heat the clarified butter / oil in a pan; add the ground spice paste and fry for 10 minutes over low heat. Then add the cashewnut paste and salt and cook for another 4-5 minutes.

◆ Add the chicken pieces and cook until the colour changes. Adding water, bring to a boil. Reduce heat and simmer until the chicken is tender. Add the remainder of the whole cashewnuts.

CHICKEN

MURGH KALONGI

(Irani style chicken cooked with onion seeds)

Serves 4-6

INGREDIENTS

700 gm	Chicken, without skin, 8 pieces
100 ml / ½ cup	Clarified butter *(ghee)* / refined oil
4	Onions, medium-sized, cut and puréed
12 gm / 2 tsp	Ginger *(adrak)* paste
12 gm / 2 tsp	Garlic *(lasan)* paste
12 gm / 4	Green chillies *(hari mirch)*, evenly chopped
4	Tomatoes *(tamatar)*, medium-sized, puréed
15 ml / 1 tbsp	Yoghurt *(dahi)*
2 gm / 1 ½ tsp	Red chilli *(lal mirch)* powder
1 gm / ½ tsp	Turmeric *(haldi)* powder
3 gm / 1 tsp	Cumin seed *(jeera)* powder
1 ½ gm / 1 tsp	Coriander seed *(dhaniya)* powder
2 ½ gm / 1½ tsp	Nigella or onion *(kalongi)* seeds
	Salt to taste

METHOD

◆ Heat the clarified butter / oil and add the onion purée; fry until translucent. Add the ginger and garlic pastes and the green chillies. Fry until dark brown. Add the tomato paste and yoghurt and cook until you get a thick consistency.
◆ Add the red chilli, turmeric, cumin seed and the coriander powders. Stir, add the chicken with the nigella seeds and salt. Stir for 2 minutes; add water and cook until the chicken is tender and the masala is thick.

Murgh Kalongi ▶

MURGH ZAFRANI

(Saffron chicken)

Serves: 4-6

INGREDIENTS

8 pieces	Chicken
100 ml / ½ cup	Clarified butter *(ghee)* / refined oil
2	Cinnamon *(dalchini)* sticks, 1"
12	Cloves *(laung)*
6	Green cardamoms *(elaichi)*
25 gm / 2 tbsp	Garlic *(lasan)*, chopped
180 gm /1½ cups	Onions *(piyaz)*, sliced
½ gm / ½ tsp	Nutmeg *(jaiphal)* powder
30 gm / 5 tsp	Ginger *(adrak)* paste
25 gm / 4 tsp	Garlic *(lasan)* paste
	Salt to taste
1 gm / ½ tsp	Red chilli *(lal mirch)* powder
500 ml / 2½ cups	Stock (chicken)
1½ gm / 1½ tsp	Saffron *(kesar)*, crushed and soaked in 4 tbsp of hot water

METHOD

◆ Heat the clarified butter / oil in an earthen pot. When hot, add the cinnamon, cloves and cardamoms. Fry until they crackle. Add the chopped garlic and fry until it turns brown.
◆ Add the onions and nutmeg powder. Sauté until the onions turn golden brown.
◆ Add the ginger and garlic pastes, the chicken pieces, salt and red chilli powder. Stir and cook till the water evaporates. Add the chicken stock and bring to a boil. Reduce heat, cover the pan and cook until the chicken becomes tender.
◆ Remove the earthen pot from the heat and cool. Take out the chicken pieces and strain the gravy through a fine strainer; collect into a pan and discard whatever is left in the strainer.
◆ Add the chicken pieces to the gravy. Simmer until the gravy is reduced to half and has a sauce-like consistency. Add the saffron. Stir and serve.

CHICKEN

MURGH SHAKOOTEE

(Spicy chicken in a thick gravy)

Serves: 6-8

INGREDIENTS

1.5 kg approx.	Chicken, skinless, cut into 10 pieces

For the spice paste:

5 gm / 10	Red chillies *(lal mirch)*, dry, soaked in hot water for 10 minutes
4 ½ gm / 1 tbsp	Coriander seed *(dhaniya)* powder
2 gm / 1 ½ tsp	Cumin *(jeera)* seeds
1 ½ gm / ½ tsp	Fenugreek seeds *(methi dana)*
10	Peppercorns *(kali mirch)*, whole
6 gm / 3 tsp	Poppy seeds *(khus khus)*
120 gm / ½ cup	Coconut *(nariyal)*, finely grated
90 gm / ¾ cup	Onions *(piyaz)*, sliced
1 ½ gm / 1 tsp	Turmeric *(haldi)* powder
½ tsp	Cardamom *(elaichi)* powder
½ tsp	Clove *(laung)* powder
½ tsp	Cinnamon *(dalchini)* powder
	Salt to taste
100 ml / ½ cup	Clarified butter *(ghee)* / refined oil
15 gm / 2½ tsp	Garlic *(lasan)* paste
15 gm / 2½ tsp	Ginger *(adrak)* paste
100 ml / ½ cup	Lemon *(nimbu)* juice

METHOD

◆ Dry roast each ingredient for the spice paste separately until brown. Blend to form a smooth paste, adding water if required.

◆ Heat the clarified butter / oil in a heavy-bottomed pan; when hot, add the spice paste, garlic and ginger pastes. Fry, stirring, until the clarified butter / oil separates from the masala.

◆ Add the chicken pieces with the salt. Stir to mix well. Cook until the water has evaporated. Add water and cook covered, until the chicken becomes tender. Add the lemon juice and mix well. The gravy should be thick and dark in colour.

Murgh Shakootee ▶

MURGH KALI MIRCH

(Peppered chicken)

Serves: 4

INGREDIENTS

600-700 gm	Chicken, without skin, cut into 8 pieces
65 gm / ¾ cup	Unsalted butter *(phika makhan)*
4 gm / 2 tbsp	Peppercorns *(kali mirch)*, coarsely ground
	Salt to taste
25 gm / 1 cup	Coriander leaves *(hara dhaniya)*, chopped

METHOD

◆ Heat the unsalted butter on low heat until it melts; add the chicken pieces and fry until they turn light brown. Add the peppercorns and salt. Stir and cook until all the water evaporates. Add ¾ cup of water and bring to a boil; reduce the heat and simmer until the chicken becomes tender and a thick gravy is obtained.

◆ Add the chopped coriander leaves, stir to mix well and cook for another 2 to 3 minutes until well blended.

SIND MURGH MUSSALLAM

(Rich, roasted whole chicken)

Serves: 4-6

INGREDIENTS

800-900 gm	Chicken, full, skinless, 1
For the marinade:	
6 gm / 1½ tsp	Salt
6 gm / 1 tsp	Bicarbonate of soda
100 ml / ½ cup	Unsalted butter / refined oil
For the stuffing:	
½ cup	Rice, cooked
2	Tomatoes *(tamatar)*, large, blanched, peeled and chopped
1	Onion *(piyaz)*, chopped
1	Ginger *(adrak)*, chopped, 1"
2	Green chillies *(hari mirch)*, chopped
2 gm / ½ tsp	Salt
1 gm / ½ tsp	Peppercorn *(kali mirch)* powder
1	Egg *(anda)*, hard-boiled, chopped
50 ml / ¼ cup	Yoghurt *(dahi)*
30 ml / 2 tbsp	Butter *(makhan)*, melted

METHOD

◆ Wash the chicken and dry with kitchen paper towels, making sure that the cavity is dry as well. Keep aside.
◆ Marinate the chicken for 1 hour.
◆ Heat 2 tablespoons of the unsalted butter / oil in a large frying pan. Add the chicken and fry until golden brown all over. Remove the pan from heat and keep aside to cool.
◆ Mix all the stuffing ingredients well. Spoon this mixture into the cavity of the chicken.
◆ Place the stuffed chicken in an oven-proof dish. Dot the chicken all over with small portions of the butter / oil. Place the dish into an oven preheated to 180⁰C / 356⁰F and roast basting regularly with butter, until the chicken becomes tender.
◆ Remove the chicken from the oven and carve into serving pieces. Serve with a small amount of the stuffing, scooped out of the cavity.

Sind Murgh Mussallam ▶

36

MURGH HARIYALI

(Coriander-mint chicken delicacy)

Serves: 4-6

INGREDIENTS

8 pieces	Chicken, without skin
6 gm / 1 tsp	Ginger *(adrak)* paste
6 gm / 1 tsp	Garlic *(lasan)* paste
150 ml / ¾ cup	Clarified butter *(ghee)* / refined oil
	Salt to taste
100 ml / ½ cup	Yoghurt *(dahi)*
150 gm / 10 tbsp	Wholemilk fudge *(khoya)*
30 gm / 10	Green chillies *(hari mirch)*, pricked all over with a fork or cocktail stick
25 gm / 1 cup	Coriander leaves *(hara dhaniya)*, fresh
15 gm / 1 cup	Mint *(pudina)* leaves, fresh chopped
240 gm / 1 cup	Coconut *(nariyal)*, grated for extracting 1 cup of coconut milk

METHOD

◆ Marinate the chicken pieces in the ginger and garlic pastes for 30 minutes.
◆ Heat the clarified butter / oil in a pan. When hot, add the chicken pieces with the marinade. Fry until lightly brown all over. Add salt, yoghurt and wholemilk fudge. Cook until the yoghurt is completely absorbed.
◆ Add the green chillies, coriander leaves and mint leaves and mix well. Add the coconut milk and simmer, keeping covered the pan, until the chicken becomes tender.

MURGH MUSSALLAM

(Whole chicken, stuffed with spices and dry fruits, cooked in a blend of yoghurt and milk)

Serves: 4-6

INGREDIENTS

600 to 700 gm	Chicken whole, skinless, 1

For the stuffing:

30 ml / 2 tbsp	Clarified butter *(ghee), durust* (see p. 21) / refined oil
4	Cloves *(laung)*
2	Cinnamon *(dalchini)* sticks, 1" each
2	Black cardamoms *(bari elaichi)*
2	Bayleaves *(tej patta)*
1 gm / ½ tsp	Mace *(javitri)*
60 gm / ½ cup	Onions *(piyaz)*, sliced
12 gm / 2 tsp	Ginger *(adrak)* paste
10	Cashewnuts *(kaju)*, ground to a paste with a little water
12 gm / 6 tsp	Poppy seeds *(khus khus)*, ground to a paste with a little water
120 gm / ½ cup	Coconut *(nariyal)*, grated, ground to a paste
6 gm / 4 tsp	Coriander seed *(dhaniya)* powder
	Salt to taste
8 gm / 10	Almonds *(badam)*, blanched, peeled and sliced
12 gm / 40	Sultanas *(kishmish)*, chopped

For the chicken:

100 ml / ½ cup	Clarified butter *(ghee)* / refined oil
300 gm / 2½ cups	Onions *(piyaz)*, sliced
12 gm / 2 tsp	Garlic *(lasan)* paste
12 gm / 2 tsp	Ginger *(adrak)* paste
4 gm / 2½ tsp	Red chilli *(lal mirch)* powder
2 gm / 1½ tsp	Coriander seed *(dhaniya)* powder
	Salt to taste
300 ml / 1½ cups	Milk
300 ml / 1½ cups	Coconut *(nariyal)* milk, thick
300 ml / 1½ cups	Yoghurt *(dahi)*

METHOD

◆ Heat the clarified butter / oil for the stuffing. Add the cloves, cinnamons, black cardamoms, bayleaves and mace. Fry until they crackle. Remove from the clarified butter / oil and grind together with a little water. Keep aside.

◆ In the same clarified butter / oil, sauté the sliced onions until they are golden brown. Remove with a slotted spoon and grind coarsely. Keep aside.

◆ In the same clarified butter / oil again, add the ginger, cashewnut, poppy seed and coconut pastes. Add the coriander powder and salt. Sauté until light brown in colour.

◆ Add the sliced almonds and sultanas. Stir and add the ground spices and ground onions. Stir well.

◆ Remove the pan from the heat and stuff the chicken with the mixture. Close the cavity with cocktail sticks. Lace the chicken with string, so that it does not lose shape and holds in the stuffing.

◆ Heat the clarified butter / oil for the chicken in a large pan. Add the sliced onions and fry until transparent; then add the ginger and garlic pastes. Fry until the water has evaporated. Add the red chilli and coriander powders. Add the chicken and fry carefully, browning it all over. Put in salt and milk. Bring to a boil and add the thick coconut milk. Simmer, keeping the pan covered, until the chicken becomes very tender but the flesh does not come off the bone and a little gravy is left. Whisk and add the yoghurt to the gravy, stir and put on *dum* (see p. 21) on very low heat until the gravy is thick and the clarified butter / oil comes to the surface.

CHICKEN

BHARWA MURGH KAJU

(Grilled chicken flavoured with cashewnut paste)

Serves: 4

CHICKEN

40

INGREDIENTS

8	Chicken breasts, boneless, flattened with a mallet

For the marinade:

25 gm / 4 tsp	Ginger *(adrak)* paste
25 gm / 4 tsp	Garlic *(lasan)* paste
40 gm / 4 tsp	Cashewnut *(kaju)* paste
1 ½ gm / 1 tsp	Red chilli *(lal mirch)* powder
2 gm / 1 tsp	Garam masala (standard, see p. 18)
	Salt to taste

For the filling: (Mix and make 8 portions)

240 gm / 1 cup	Onions *(piyaz)*, finely chopped, fried until golden brown and drained
150 gm	Wholemilk fudge *(khoya)*
18 gm / 6	Green chillies *(hari mirch)*, chopped finely
4 gm / ¼ cup	Mint *(pudina)* leaves, finely chopped
12½ gm / ½ cup	Coriander leaves *(hara dhaniya)*, finely chopped
30 ml / 2 tbsp	Lemon *(nimbu)* juice

For the gravy:

150 ml / ¾ cup	Clarified butter *(ghee)*, durust (see p. 21) / refined oil
300 gm / 1½ cups	Onions *(piyaz)*, finely chopped
25 gm / 4 tsp	Ginger *(adrak)* paste
25 gm / 4 tsp	Garlic *(lasan)* paste
125 gm / ½ cup	Cashewnut *(kaju)* paste
300 ml / 1½ cups	Yoghurt *(dahi)*, whisked
3 gm / 1 ½ tsp	Garam masala, (fragrant, see p. 18)
½ gm / ½ tsp	Saffron *(kesar)*, soaked in 3 tbsp warm milk

METHOD

◆ Marinate the chicken breasts for half an hour.

◆ Lay out each chicken breast. Place one portion of the filling and roll the breast over it.

◆ Oil a baking dish and lay the rolled breasts of chicken with the loose ends resting on the tray. This will help in sealing the rolls. Put the tray in the oven and grill until the breasts are golden brown. Remove from the oven and keep aside.

◆ To make the gravy heat the clarified butter, *durust* (see p. 21) / oil in a large pan. Add the onions. Sauté until they are translucent. Add the ginger and garlic pastes and stir until the water evaporates and they change their colour. Reduce heat; add the cashewnut paste and fry until well blended and the colour changes. Add the yoghurt. Stir and simmer until a sauce-like consistency is achieved. Add the garam masala and the saffron milk. Stir and mix well.

◆ Add the chicken breasts and half a cup of water. Simmer for 10 minutes, coating the breasts with the gravy.

MURGH KI BARI

(A unique Nepalese preparation of chicken mince balls, cooked in mustard oil)

Serves: 4-6

INGREDIENTS

6	Chicken breasts, boneless
1 ½ gm / 1 tsp	Anise pepper *(chakri phool)* powder
6 gm / 2 tsp	Cumin seed *(jeera)* powder
6 gm / 1 tsp	Bicarbonate of soda
1 gm / ½ tsp	Red chilli *(lal mirch)* powder
	Salt to taste
100 ml / 1 cup	Mustard oil *(sarson ka tel)*
40	Garlic *(lasan)* cloves
25 gm / 15-20	Green chillies *(hari mirch)*, slit

METHOD

◆ Cube the chicken and put in a high-speed blender. Blend the chicken for about 2 minutes or until it becomes a purée. Add the anise powder, cumin seed powder, bicarbonate of soda, red chilli powder and salt and blend for another 30 seconds. Remove the mixture and make balls about the size of a golf ball each, using water or mustard oil on your hands to avoid the mixture from sticking.

◆ Heat the mustard oil until it smokes; reduce heat to half and gently put the chicken balls in and fry until golden. Remove with a slotted spoon and keep aside. Cut a cross (x) on one side of the fried balls with a sharp knife going half way down the ball.

◆ Ten minutes before serving, heat the oil once again and add the garlic and green chillies and fry for 1 minute. Then add the fried chicken balls and with a spoon, pour the hot oil over them until the cut opens up like petals. Fry until they are golden brown all over. Serve in the frying pan with the oil.

42

CHICKEN

NIHARI

(Tender meat shanks infused with garlic)

Serves: 4

INGREDIENTS

500 gm	Lamb / mutton shanks
50 gm / 8 tsp	Garlic *(lasan)* paste, ground very fine
For the masala:	
60 gm / 6 tbsp	White butter *(safed makhan)*
3 gm / 2 tsp	Red chilli *(lal mirch)* powder
12 gm / 8 tsp	Coriander seed *(dhaniya)* powder
36 gm / 6 tsp	Ginger *(adrak)* paste
	Salt to taste
133 ml / 1⅓ cups	Water
18 gm / 3 tsp	Refined flour *(maida)*
100 ml / ½ cup	Milk
For the baghar (flavouring):	
60 gm / 6 tbsp	White butter *(safed makhan)* / clarified butter *(ghee)*
60 gm / ½ cup	Onions *(piyaz)*, finely sliced
6	Cloves *(laung)*, powdered
6	Green cardamoms *(elaichi)*, powdered
12	Peppercorns *(kali mirch)*, powdered
2	Cinnamon *(dalchini)* sticks, 2"
20 ml / 4 tsp	Lemon *(nimbu)* juice

METHOD

◆ Boil the lamb / mutton in 1 cup of water for 15 minutes. Drain the meat pieces and keep aside, reserving the stock. Add the finely ground garlic paste to the stock and stir well. Use later to *bhunao* (see p. 21).

◆ **For the masala,** heat the white butter; add the red chilli powder, coriander seed powder and ginger paste. Add salt and *bhunao,* adding the garlic stock a little at a time. Continue until the stock is consumed. Add the meat pieces and 1 ⅓ cups of water.

◆ Dilute the refined flour in milk and add to the meat. Cook on very low heat, stirring regularly until the meat becomes tender. Remove from heat and keep aside.

◆ **For the *baghar*** (see p. 20), in a separate pan, heat the white butter / clarified butter; add the sliced onions and sauté until golden brown. Remove and make a paste. Add the onion paste to the meat and stir well.

◆ Reduce heat to low and in the same butter, add the clove powder, cardamom powder, peppercorn powder and cinnamon sticks. Immediately add to the meat *(if fried for long, the powdered masalas will burn).* Stir.

◆ Add the lemon juice to the meat. Return the pan to the heat and bring to a boil, stirring regularly.

Nihari ▶

GOSHT KA SALAN

(Spiced meat cooked in milk)

Serves: 6-8

INGREDIENTS

1 kg	Lamb / mutton
200 ml / 1 cup	Clarified butter *(ghee)* / refined oil
6	Cloves *(laung)*
2	Cinnamon *(dalchini)* sticks, 1"
1 ½ gm / 1 tsp	Red chilli *(lal mirch)* powder
1 gm / 20	Peppercorns *(kali mirch)*
3 gm / 1 tsp	Sugar
2 gm / 1 tsp	Garam masala (standard, see p. 18)
250 ml / 1¼ cups	Full cream milk
300 ml / 1½ cups	Water
	Salt to taste

METHOD

◆ Heat the clarified butter *(ghee)* / oil in an earthen pot. Add the cloves, cinnamon sticks, red chilli powder, peppercorns, meat and salt. Fry until the meat turns light brown in colour.

◆ Add the sugar and stir. Then add the water. Bring to a boil, reduce the heat and simmer until the meat becomes tender and the water is absorbed.

◆ Add the garam masala. Stir, reduce the heat further and add the milk. Cook uncovered for a further 10-12 minutes.

MUGHLAI KORMA

(Lamb / mutton curry cooked in the royal Mughal style)

Serves: 4

INGREDIENTS

500 gm	Lamb / mutton
100 ml / ½ cup	Clarified butter *(ghee)* / refined oil
4	Cloves *(laung)*
6	Green cardamoms *(elaichi)*, cracked
2	Cinnamon *(dalchini)*, sticks
18 gm / 3 tsp	Garlic *(lasan)* paste
18 gm / 3 tsp	Ginger *(adrak)* paste
18 gm / 3 tsp	Green chilli *(hari mirch)* paste
2 gm / 2 tsp	Green coriander leaf *(hara dhaniya)* paste
100 ml / ½ cup	Yoghurt *(dahi)*, whisked
	Salt to taste
50 gm / 2 tbsp	Onions *(piyaz)*, chopped, roasted and ground to a paste
125 gm / ½ cup	Almond *(badam)* paste
2 gm / 1 tsp	Peppercorn *(kali mirch)* powder
½ gm / ½ tsp	Saffron *(kesar)*, dissolved in 3 tsp warm milk

METHOD

◆ Heat the clarified butter / oil in an earthen pot; add the cloves, cardamoms and cinnamon. When they crackle, add the garlic, ginger, green chilli and green coriander pastes. Fry until light brown.

◆ Add the meat with the yoghurt. Add salt and cook well on low heat, until the clarified butter / oil leaves the masala. Add enough water, so that very little is left by the time the meat becomes tender.

◆ Add the onion and almond pastes, peppercorn powder and the saffron. Stir and heat for 5 minutes. Remove from heat.

GOSHT AUR GOBI DO PIYAZA

(Cauliflower and meat—a two-in-one delight)

Serves: 4

INGREDIENTS

500 gm	Lamb / mutton, boneless, cut into cubes
12 gm / 2 tsp	Garlic *(lasan)* paste
12 gm / 2 tsp	Ginger *(adrak)* paste
3 gm / 2 tsp	Red chilli *(lal mirch)* powder
4½ gm / 1½ tsp	Cumin seed *(jeera)* powder
4 gm / 2 tsp	Peppercorn *(kali mirch)* powder
	Salt to taste
100 ml / ½ cup	Clarified butter *(ghee)* / refined oil
300 gm / 1½ cup	Onions *(piyaz)*, chopped
100 ml / ½ cup	Yoghurt *(dahi)*, whisked
1	Cauliflower *(phool gobi)*, small, only the florets

METHOD

◆ Marinate the meat in the garlic and ginger pastes, red chilli powder, cumin seed powder, peppercorn powder and salt. Keep aside for 15 minutes.

◆ Heat the clarified butter / oil in an earthen pot add the chopped onions and sauté until light brown. Reduce the heat and add the yoghurt, stirring all the time, until well blended. Add the marinated meat pieces. Cook on low heat until all the water evaporates and the meat turns brown in colour. Add one cup of water and cook until the meat becomes tender and a little water remains.

◆ Add the cauliflower to the meat and stir to mix well. Cover the earthen pot and cook without stirring until the cauliflower is done.

L A M B

AAB GOSHT

(Lamb / mutton curry cooked in milk)

Serves: 6-8

INGREDIENTS

1 kg	Lamb / mutton
1 lt	Water
7 ½ gm / 5 tsp	Aniseed *(saunf)* powder
5	Garlic *(lasan)* cloves, crushed
2 gm / 1 tsp	Dry ginger powder *(sonth)*
	Salt to taste
1 lt	Milk
6	Green caradmoms *(elaichi)*, split open
25 gm / 1 tbsp	Onion *(piyaz)* paste, fried
6 gm / 1 tbsp	Peppercorn *(kali mirch)* powder
100 ml / ½ cup	Clarified butter *(ghee)* / refined oil

METHOD

◆ Boil the lamb / mutton in the water with the aniseed powder, garlic cloves, dry ginger powder and salt. Boil until the meat is tender. Remove the meat pieces from the stock; sieve the stock and put into another pan.

◆ In a separate pan, boil the milk with the cardamoms. Boil until the milk is reduced by half. Add the onion paste, the peppercorn powder and clarified butter / oil. Add the meat and the stock. Mix well and bring to a boil. Continue to boil uncovered for 5-7 minutes and then reduce the heat to low and simmer for another 10 minutes.

▲ *Aab Gosht*

MAANS ACHAARI

(Lamb / mutton laced with treacle)

Serves: 4

INGREDIENTS

500 gm	Mutton / lamb pieces, cleaned of fat

For the marinade:

1 gm / ½ tsp	Turmeric *(haldi)* powder
6 gm / 1 ½ tsp	Salt

For cooking:

100 ml / ½ cup	Mustard oil *(sarson ka tel)*
8	Red chillies *(lal mirch)*, whole, dried
1 gm / ¼ tsp	Asafoetida *(hing)*
4½ gm / 1½ tsp	Black mustard seeds *(sarson)*
5	Cloves *(laung)*
1½ gm / 1 tsp	Red chilli *(lal mirch)* powder
2 gm / 1 tsp	Cumin seeds *(jeera)*
1 ½ gm / 1 tsp	Nigella *(kalonji)* seeds
30 ml / 2 tbsp	Treacle or brown sugar, dissolved in ½ cup of hot water
12 gm / 2 tsp	Ginger *(adrak)* paste
12 gm / 2 tsp	Garlic *(lasan)* paste
2	Onions *(piyaz)*, finely sliced, fried till golden brown and made into a paste
30 ml / 2 tbsp	Lemon *(nimbu)* juice
100 ml / ½ cup	Yoghurt *(dahi)*, whisked

METHOD

◆ Mix the meat with the turmeric and salt and boil in 2 cups of water. Cover and simmer until the meat is tender. Drain the meat and reserve the stock.

◆ Heat the mustard oil in a heavy-bottomed vessel until it smokes. Reduce the heat and add the whole, dry red chillies. Fry until they are black in colour and then discard them.

◆ In the same oil add the asafoetida, mustard seeds and the cloves. Stir until they crackle; add the boiled meat, red chilli powder, cumin seeds, nigella seeds, treacle syrup, ginger and garlic pastes. Stir to mix well. Add the fried onion paste, raise the heat and *bhunao* (see p. 21) with the reserved stock, until the meat is brown in colour. Add the lemon juice. Simmer for 2 minutes.

◆ Add the whisked yoghurt; stir well and cook until the oil surfaces.

Maans Achaari ▶

LAL MAANS

('Red' meat)

Serves: 6-8

INGREDIENTS

1 ½ kg	Lamb / mutton, cut into pieces
200 ml / 1 cup	Clarified butter *(ghee)* / refined oil
60 gm / ½ cup	Garlic *(lasan)*, finely chopped
180 gm / 1½ cups	Onions *(piyaz)*, sliced
5 gm / 10	Black cardamoms *(bari elaichi)*

For the yoghurt mixture, whisk and keep:

200 ml / 1 cup	Yoghurt *(dahi)*, whisked
12 gm / 40	Red chillies *(lal mirch)*, whole, slit and deseeded
2 gm / 1 ½ tsp	Cumin seeds *(jeera)*, roasted
6 gm / 4 tsp	Coriander seed *(dhaniya)* powder
1 gm / ½ tsp	Turmeric *(haldi)* powder
	Salt to taste
9 gm / 6 tsp	Red chilli *(lal mirch)* powder dissloved in ½ cup water

METHOD

◆ Heat the clarified butter / oil; add garlic and fry until golden brown. Add the onions with the black cardamoms and cook until golden brown.

◆ Add the meat and *bhunao* (see p. 21), adding a few tablespoons of water until the meat is reddish brown in colour. Add the yoghurt mixture and cook, stirring until the liquid has dried. Add water and bring to a boil. Cover and simmer until the meat is tender, stirring occasionally. Add the dissolved red chilli water and stir to mix well. Reduce heat and simmer for 5 minutes.

PUNJABI GOSHT

(Meat curry cooked with a hint of dry mango powder)

Serves: 4

INGREDIENTS

500 gm	Lamb / mutton, cut into cubes

To make a paste:

18 gm / 6	Green chillies *(hari mirch)*
10	Garlic *(lasan)* cloves, chopped
25 gm / 3 tsp	Ginger *(adrak)*, chopped
12 gm / 3 tbsp	Coriander leaves *(hara dhaniya)*, chopped
75 ml / ⅓ cup	Clarified butter *(ghee)* / refined oil
2	Onions *(piyaz)*, sliced evenly
3 gm / 1½ tsp	Garam masala (see p. 18)
3 gm / 2 tsp	Turmeric *(haldi)* powder
3 gm / 1½ tsp	Dry mango powder *(amchur)*
	Salt to taste

METHOD

◆ Make a paste of the green chillies, chopped garlic, ginger and coriander leaves and keep aside.

◆ Heat the clarified butter / oil; add the sliced onions and fry until golden in colour.

◆ Add the paste and cook until aromatic.

◆ Add the meat with the garam masala, turmeric powder, dry mango powder and salt. Stir for one minute; then add enough water to cover the meat and cook covered until the meat becomes tender and the gravy is thick.

Punjabi Gosht ▶

GOSHT DO RUKH KA

(Spicy lamb / mutton)

Serves: 4

INGREDIENTS

500 gm	Lamb / mutton, cut into pieces
100 ml / ½ cup	Clarified butter *(ghee)* / refined oil
240 gm / 1 cup	Onions *(piyaz)*, finely chopped
	Salt to taste
15 gm / 2½ tsp	Ginger *(adrak)* paste
15 gm / 2½ tsp	Garlic *(lasan)* paste
3	Green cardamoms *(elaichi)*, cracked
2	Black cardamoms *(bari elaichi)*, cracked
3	Cloves *(laung)*
2	Cinnamon *(dalchini)* sticks, 1"
1 ½ gm / ¾ tsp	Peppercorn *(kali mirch)* powder
1 gm / ¾ tsp	Red chilli *(lal mirch)* powder
1 gm / ¾ tsp	Turmeric *(haldi)* powder
4 gm / 2½ tsp	Coriander *(dhaniya)* powder
¾ cup	Tomatoes *(tamatar)*, purée
7½ gm / 2½ tsp	Cumin seed *(jeera)* powder
6 gm / ¼ cup	Coriander leaves *(hara dhaniya)*, chopped

METHOD

◆ Heat the clarified butter / oil; add the onions and fry until brown. Add the meat with the salt. Reduce heat and fry until the water evaporates and the meat turns light brown. Add the ginger and garlic pastes. *Bhunao* (see p. 21), adding a few tablespoons of water, until the meat becomes deep brown in colour. Add the green and black cardamoms, cloves, cinnamon sticks and peppercorn powder. Stir for 15 seconds. Add water, bring to a boil and simmer, keeping the pan covered, until the meat becomes tender and some water remains.

◆ Add the red chilli powder, turmeric and coriander powders, tomato purée, cumin seed powder and coriander leaves and cook until well blended. Add water if a thick gravy is required.

DANIWAL KORMA

(Richly spiced lamb / mutton curry)

Serves: 6-8

INGREDIENTS

1 kg	Lamb / mutton, cut into pieces
150 ml / ¾ cup	Clarified butter *(ghee)* / refined oil
400 ml / 2 cups	Yoghurt *(dahi)*, whisked
480 gm / 2 cups	Onions *(piyaz)*, chopped
4 gm / 2 tsp	Dry ginger powder *(sonth)*
3 gm / 2 tsp	Aniseed *(saunf)* powder
4½ gm / 3 tsp	Coriander seed *(dhaniya)* powder
4 gm / 2 tsp	Peppercorn *(kali mirch)* powder
1 ½ gm / 1 tsp	Turmeric *(haldi)* powder
	Salt to taste
35 gm / 1½ cups	Coriander leaves *(hara dhaniya)*, chopped coarsely

METHOD

◆ Heat the clarified butter / oil in an earthen pot; add the yoghurt and onions. Cook until there is a uniform consistency and colour.
◆ Add the meat pieces and stir until well mixed. Add the dry ginger powder, aniseed powder, coriander seed powder, peppercorn powder, turmeric powder and salt. Add water and bring to a boil. Reduce heat.
◆ Add the coriander leaves and stir; cover and simmer until the meat becomes tender.

Daniwal Korma ▶

VINDALOO

(Spicy Goan meat delight)

Serves: 6

INGREDIENTS

750 gm	Lamb / mutton, cut into pieces
200 ml / 1 cup	Malt vinegar *(sirka)*
2 gm / 1 tsp	Peppercorns *(kali mirch)*, coarsely ground
3 gm / 1 tsp	Sugar
5	Green cardamoms *(elaichi)*, cracked
18 gm / 6	Green chillies *(hari mirch)*, finely chopped
5	Cloves *(laung)*
10	Red chillies *(lal mirch)*, whole, dry
10	Cinnamon *(dalchini)* sticks, 1" each
1½ gm / ½ tsp	Cumin seed *(jeera)* powder
1 ½ gm / 1 tsp	Turmeric *(haldi)* powder
36 gm / 2 tbsp	Ginger *(adrak)* paste
18 gm / 1 tbsp	Garlic *(lasan)* paste
100 ml / ½ cup	Clarified butter *(ghee)* / refined oil
120 gm / ½ cup	Onions *(piyaz)*, chopped
	Salt to taste

METHOD

◆ Mix half the vinegar with the pounded peppercorns, sugar, cracked cardamoms, green chillies and cloves. Marinate the lamb / mutton in this mixture for at least 12 hours or overnight.
◆ Make a paste in a blender with the whole red chillies, cinnamon sticks, cumin seed powder, turmeric, ginger and garlic pastes, the remainder of the vinegar and a little water.
◆ Heat the clarified butter / oil in a pan; add the onions and sauté until brown; Add the paste and cook until the oil rises to the surface.
◆ Add the meat with the marinade and fry until the water evaporates and the meat turns deep brown in colour. Add water and bring to a boil. Cover the pan and simmer until the meat is tender.

L A M B

GHAR KE CHAAMP

(Vinegar-flavoured ribs)

Serves: 6-8

INGREDIENTS

1 kg	Lamb / mutton ribs, double
100 ml / ½ cup	Clarified butter *(ghee)* / refined oil
720 gm / 3 cups	Onions *(piyaz)*, minced
2	Cinnamon *(dalchini)* / sticks, 1"
	Salt to taste
6 gm / 2 tsp	Sugar
1 ½ gm / 1 tsp	Red chilli *(lal mirch)* powder
100 ml / ½ cup	Malt vinegar *(sirka)*
2 gm / 1 tsp	Garam masala (standard, see p. 18)

METHOD

◆ Heat the oil in a deep-bottomed vessel; add the onions and cinnamon sticks. Sauté until the onions become translucent. Add the ribs, stir and add one litre of warm water, salt, sugar, red chilli powder, vinegar and garam masala, and bring to a boil.

◆ Reduce the heat to low and cover the pan. Cook until the ribs are tender and very little gravy remains.

Ghar Ke Chaamp ▶

L A M B

ELAICHI GOSHT

(Cardamom-flavoured meat)

Serves: 6-8

INGREDIENTS

1 kg	Lamb / mutton, cut into 1" pieces
For the paste:	
2	Onions *(piyaz)*, medium-sized, cut into 4 pieces each
20	Garlic *(lasan)* cloves
30 gm / 10	Green chillies *(hari mirch)*
12 gm / 15	Almonds *(badam)*, blanched, peeled, ground
2 gm / 1 tsp	Poppy seeds *(khus khus)*, ground
65 gm / ¾ cup	Unsalted butter *(makhan)*
10	Green cardamoms *(elaichi)*, cracked
100 ml / 1 cup	Yoghurt *(dahi)*
	Salt to taste
300 ml / 2½ cups	Water
200 ml / 1 cup	Cream
4 gm / 2 tsp	Cardamom seed *(elaichi)* powder
4 gm / 1 tbsp	Coriander leaves *(hara dhaniya)*, evenly chopped

METHOD

◆ Blend the ingredients for the paste with a little water to make a smooth paste.

◆ Heat the unsalted butter, add the green cardamoms and stir. Then add the paste and stir until it changes colour. Add the meat with the yoghurt, salt and 2 ½ cups of water. Reduce heat and cover. Cook, stirring occasionally, until the meat becomes tender.

◆ Reduce the heat further, add the cream and the cardamom powder; bring to a boil and remove from heat immediately. Stir once, garnish with coriander leaves before serving.

BHOPALI KORMA

(Meat slow cooked in its own marinade)

Serves: 4

INGREDIENTS

500 gm	Lamb / mutton cubed
45 gm / 15	Green chillies *(hari mirch)*, slit and deseeded
240 gm / 2 cups	Onions *(piyaz)*, very thinly sliced
400 ml / 2 cups	Yoghurt *(dahi)*, whisked
25 gm / 1 cup	Coriander leaves *(hara dhaniya)*, fresh, chopped
40 gm / 5 tsp	Ginger *(adrak)*, shredded
12 gm / 3 tsp	Garlic *(lasan)*, finely chopped
3 gm / 1 tsp	Cumin seed *(jeera)* powder
	Salt to taste
100 ml / ½ cup	Clarified butter *(ghee)* / refined oil

METHOD

◆ Mix all the ingredients, except the clarified butter / oil with the lamb / mutton.
◆ In a heavy-bottomed pan, heat the clarified butter / oil and put the meat with the marinade into it. Mix well and bring to a boil rapidly. Reduce heat to low and cover the pan with a tight lid or put a weight on the lid to seal it. Cook for at least 1 hour.
◆ Open the lid, stir and serve immediately.

56

Bhopali Korma ▶

SIKA PIYAZ AUR GOSHT

(Baked onion meat speciality)

Serves: 4

INGREDIENTS

500 gm	Lamb / mutton, boneless, cut into 1" x 1" cubes
4	Onions *(piyaz)*, medium, whole with the skin
½	Coconut *(nariyal)*, grated
12 gm / 2 tsp	Ginger *(adrak)* paste
12 gm / 2 tsp	Garlic *(lasan)* paste

Dry roast separately and grind together into a fine paste:

6 gm / 2 tsp	Sesame seeds *(til)*, roasted
4 ½ gm / 2 tsp	Poppy seeds *(khus khus)*, roasted
3 gm / 2 tsp	Cumin seeds *(jeera)*, roasted
	Salt to taste
100 ml / ½ cup	Clarified butter *(ghee)* / refined oil
100 gm	Tamarind *(imli)* pulp, diluted in one cup of hot water, and juice extracted through a sieve

METHOD

◆ Preheat the oven to 180^0 C / 356^0 F. Put the onions in a small baking tray and place in the oven to bake until done (about 20 minutes).
◆ Remove the onions from the oven and cool. Remove the outer skin of the onions and make a paste with the grated coconut, ginger and garlic pastes and the roasted spice paste. Grind until a smooth paste is formed. Mix this paste with the meat pieces. Add salt.
◆ Heat the clarified butter / oil in a pan; add the meat with all the pastes and fry until dark brown. Add the tamarind extract. Stir and add enough water to cook on low heat, until it has a thick gravy and the meat becomes tender.

KEEMA HARIYALI

(Minced meat blended with the goodness of greens)

Serves: 6

LAMB

INGREDIENTS

750 gm	Lamb / mutton, minced
25 gm / ¾ cup	Spinach *(palak)*, washed, chopped and boiled till tender
6 gm / 1½ tbsp	Mint leaves *(pudina)*, chopped
10 gm / 2½ tbsp	Coriander leaves *(hara dhaniya)*, chopped
100 ml / ½ cup	Clarified butter *(ghee)* / refined oil
4	Cloves *(laung)*
2	Green cardamoms *(elaichi)*
1	Cinnamon *(dalchini)* stick, 1"
18 gm / 1 tbsp	Garlic *(lasan)* paste
18 gm / 1 tbsp	Ginger *(adrak)* paste
180 gm / ¾ cup	Onions *(piyaz)*, chopped
12 gm / 4	Green chillies *(hari mirch)*, whole with the stems removed
	Salt to taste
200 ml / 1 cup	Yoghurt *(dahi)*, whisked
1 gm / ½ tsp	Garam masala (standard, see p. 18)

METHOD

◆ Make a paste in a blender of the spinach, mint leaves and coriander leaves, using a little water.

◆ Heat the clarified butter / oil in a wok *(kadhai)*. When hot, add the cloves, green cardamoms and cinnamon. Fry for 1 minute; then add the garlic and ginger pastes. Cook until the water evaporates. Add the onions and green chillies. Mix well.

◆ Add the mince meat, salt and cook until the moisture evaporates. Add the yoghurt and cook until it is reduced by half and the meat becomes tender.

◆ Add the spinach paste and garam masala. Simmer and stir for 2 to 3 minutes.

Keema Hariyali ▶

MOPLAH GOSHT

(Tangy lamb / mutton with coconut milk)

Serves: 6-8

INGREDIENTS

1 kg	Lamb / mutton, cubed
For the marinade:	
2½ gm / 1½ tsp	Turmeric *(haldi)* powder
3 gm / 2 tsp	Red chilli *(lal mirch)* powder, Salt to taste
8	Peppercorns *(kali mirch)*
2	Cinnamon *(dalchini)* sticks, 2"
300 ml / 1½ cups	Meat stock
100 ml / ½ cup	Clarified butter *(ghee)* / refined oil
180 gm / ¾ cup	Onions *(piyaz)*, chopped
Dry roast and grind to a fine powder:	
2	Red chillies *(lal mirch)*, whole, dry
4 gm / 2 tsp	Coriander seeds *(dhaniya)*
1	Cinnamon *(dalchini)* stick, 1"
6 each	Cloves *(laung)*, Peppercorns *(kali mirch)*
200 ml / 1 cup	Thick coconut milk of 1 full coconut
100 ml / ½ cup	Tamarind *(imli)* juice
1 ½ gm / 1 tsp	Aniseed *(saunf)* powder

METHOD

◆ Marinate the meat in the turmeric powder, red chilli powder and salt for half an hour.

◆ Boil two cups of water, add the peppercorns and cinnamon stick. Boil for a minute, then add the meat to the boiling water. Boil for another 10 minutes. Remove the meat and keep the stock. Add water to make 1 ½ cups.

◆ Heat the clarified butter / oil in a pan and sauté the onions until light brown. Add the ground spices and stir until aromatic. Add the boiled meat and all the stock. Cook until the meat is tender.

◆ Add the coconut milk and tamarind juice and simmer until the gravy becomes thick.

◆ Sprinkle the aniseed powder all over and mix well.

RAAN MUSSALLAM

(Basted leg of lamb / mutton, cooked the Avadhi way)

Serves: 6-8

INGREDIENTS

1 kg	Lamb / mutton, whole leg
100 ml / ½ cup	Yoghurt (dahi)
60 gm / ½ cup	Onions (piyaz), sliced and fried, ground to a paste
9 gm / 6 tsp	Red chilli (lal mirch) powder
9 gm / 6 tsp	Coriander seed (dhaniya) powder
3 gm / 1½ tsp	Garam masala (fragrant, see p. 18)
8 gm / 4 tsp	Peppercorn (kali mirch) powder
20 gm / 2½ tbsp	Parched gram (bhuna chana) powder
10	Almonds (badam), blanched, peeled and ground to a paste
25 gm / 4 tsp	Ginger (adrak) paste
3 gm / 1½ tsp	Green cardamom seed (elaichi) powder
1" x 1"	Mace (javitri), powdered
25 gm / 4 tsp	Papaya (papita), raw, paste
30 gm / 2 tbsp	Wholemilk fudge (khoya)
30 ml / 2 tbsp	Vetivier (kewra) essence
	Salt to taste
100 ml / ½ cup	Clarified butter (ghee), durust (see p. 21) / refined oil

METHOD

◆ Remove the white membrane from the leg of lamb; prick with a fork all over. Make 2-3 incisions across the leg, going down to the bone on both sides.

◆ Marinate the leg of meat in all the ingredients, except the clarified butter / oil. Spread the marinade evenly. Prick all over with a fork once again, pushing the marinade into the cuts. Keep covered for 2 hours.

◆ Place the leg in an oven-proof, wide pan. Heat the clarified butter / oil in another pan and pour it around and over the leg. Baste the leg with the clarified butter / oil. Put the pan into an oven, preheated to 170° C / 338° F. Cook for two hours, basting with clarified butter occasionally. Cook until the meat is tender and brown in colour.

Raan Mussallam ▶

GOSHT SADAGI

(Succulent lamb / mutton pieces)

Serves: 4

INGREDIENTS

½ kg	Lamb / mutton, cut into pieces
18 gm / 3 tsp	Garlic (lasan) paste
18 gm / 3 tsp	Ginger (adrak) paste
4 ½ gm / 1½ tsp	Cumin seed (jeera) powder
1 ½ gm / 1 tsp	Turmeric (haldi) powder
2 gm / 1½ tsp	Red chilli (lal mirch) powder
2 gm / 1 tsp	Peppercorn (kali mirch) powder
100 ml / ½ cup	Clarified butter (ghee) / refined oil
180 gm / ¾ cup	Onions (piyaz), finely chopped
100 ml / ½ cup	Yoghurt (dahi), whisked
50 gm / 2½ tbsp	Tomato (tamatar) purée (see p. 24)
2 gm / 1 tsp	Garam masala (see p. 18)
	Salt to taste

METHOD

◆ Marinate the lamb / mutton in the garlic and ginger pastes, cumin seed powder, turmeric, red chilli powder and peppercorn powder for half an hour.

◆ Heat the clarified butter / oil and fry the onions until brown. Add the meat and cook until brown. Add a few tablespoons of water, in case it sticks to the bottom.

◆ Put in the yoghurt, tomato purée and salt. Stir and cook until the water evaporates. Add water and cook until the meat is tender. Sprinkle the garam masala and stir to mix well.

BADAMI GOSHT

(Almond meat)

Serves: 4

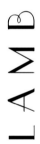

INGREDIENTS

500 gm	Lamb / mutton, cubed
45 gm / ½ cup	Unsalted butter *(phika makhan)*
180 gm / ¾ cup	Onions *(piyaz)*, finely chopped
9 gm / 1 ½ tsp	Ginger *(adrak)* paste
9 gm / 1 ½ tsp	Garlic *(lasan)* paste
100 ml / ½ cup	Yoghurt *(dahi)*, whisked
12 gm / 4	Green chillies *(hari mirch)*, chopped
	Salt to taste
100 ml / ½ cup	Tomato *(tamatar)* purée
25 / 2 tbsp	Almond *(badam)* paste
2 gm / 1 tsp	Green cardamom seed *(elaichi)* powder
½ gm / ½ tsp	Saffron *(kesar)*, dissolved in 2 tbsp of warm milk
30 ml / 2 tbsp	Cream
2 tbsp	Almonds *(badam)*, blanched, peeled and sliced for garnishing

METHOD

◆ Heat the unsalted butter; add the meat with the onions, ginger and garlic pastes, yoghurt, green chillies and salt. Cook, stirring regularly, until the water evaporates. Add the tomato purée. Mix well and cook for 1 minute. Add water and bring to a boil. Then reduce heat and keep the pan covered, until the meat becomes tender.

◆ Add the almond paste, cardamom seed powder and saffron milk. Stir, add the cream and heat thoroughly. Before serving, sprinkle the sliced almonds on top as a garnish.

CHAAMP LOABDAR

(Tender fried ribs)

Serves: 4-6

INGREDIENTS

2	Lamb / mutton bone ribs, cut into 8 pieces

Marinate the ribs and keep for 45 minutes:

½	Lemon *(nimbu)*, juice
9 gm / 2 tsp	Salt
3 gm / 2 tsp	Red chilli *(lal mirch)* powder
100 ml / ½ cup	Clarified butter *(ghee)* / refined oil
120 gm / ½ cup	Onions *(piyaz)*, finely chopped
6 gm / 1 tsp	Garlic *(lasan)* paste
6 gm / 1 tsp	Ginger *(adrak)* paste

Mix together:

3 gm / 1 tsp	Cumin seed *(jeera)* powder
1 gm / ½ tsp	Fenugreek seed *(methi dana)* powder
12 ½ gm / 1 tbsp	Pomegranate seed *(anardana)* powder
1 ½ gm / 1 tsp	Red chilli *(lal mirch)* powder
200 ml / 1 cup	Yoghurt *(dahi)*
½ gm / ½ tsp	Saffron *(kesar)* soaked in 2 tbsp hot water for 10 minutes
4 gm / 1 tbsp	Coriander leaves *(hara dhaniya)*, chopped

METHOD

◆ Heat the clarified butter / oil in a large frying pan; when hot, fry the marinated ribs, a few at a time, for a few minutes or until they are evenly browned. Remove the ribs and keep aside.

◆ In the same clarified butter / oil (add more if necessary), add the onions, garlic and ginger pastes and fry until the onions turn golden brown.

◆ Add the mixture to the onions and cook until the mixture comes to a boil. Add the fried ribs and mix well until they are well coated. Reduce the heat to low and cover the pan and cook for 10-15 minutes, stirring occasionally.

◆ Uncover the pan and cook the ribs for a further 20-25 minutes or until the gravy becomes very thick and the ribs tender. Garnish with the chopped coriander leaves.

SEB AUR TAMATAR GOSHT

(Apple and tomato-flavoured meat)

Serves: 4

INGREDIENTS

500 gm	Lamb / mutton, boneless
100 ml / ½ cup	Clarified butter *(ghee)* / refined oil
60 gm / ½ cup	Onions *(piyaz)*, sliced
12 gm / 2 tsp	Garlic *(lasan)* paste
12 gm / 2 tsp	Ginger *(adrak)* paste
3 gm / 2 tsp	Red chilli *(lal mirch)* powder
	Salt to taste
1 ½	Green apples *(hare seb)*, cored and quartered
1 ½	Tomatoes *(tamatar)*, quartered

METHOD

◆ Heat the clarified butter / oil; add the sliced onions and fry until light brown. Add the meat and cook until the water evaporates and the meat turns light brown in colour.

◆ Add the garlic and ginger pastes, red chilli powder and salt. Fry until brown; add water and bring to a boil. Cover and simmer until the meat becomes tender and the water evaporates once again.

◆ Add the green apples and tomatoes. Stir and cook until the clarified butter / oil separates from the masala, the apples become tender and the tomatoes are mixed well with the masala.

▲ *Seb Aur Tamatar Gosht*

GOSHT LAZEEZ

(Meat with the subtle flavour of black pepper and coconut milk)

Serves: 6-8

INGREDIENTS

1 kg	Lamb / mutton pieces
150 ml / ¾ cup	Clarified butter / refined oil
4	Red chillies *(lal mirch)*, dry
300 gm / 1½ cups	Onions *(piyaz)*, chopped
12 gm / 2 tsp	Ginger *(adrak)* paste
2 gm / 1½ tsp	Red chilli *(lal mirch)* powder
1 gm / ¾ tsp	Turmeric *(haldi)* powder
4 gm / 2½ tsp	Coriander seed *(dhaniya)* powder
	Salt to taste
12 gm / 2 tsp	Garlic *(lasan)* paste added to ¾ cup warm water
400 ml / 2 tsp	Coconut *(nariyal)* milk, thick
2 gm / 1 tsp	Peppercorns *(kali mirch)*, coarsely ground to a powder
15 ml / 1 tbsp	Lemon *(nimbu)* juice

METHOD

◆ Heat the clarified butter / oil in a heavy-bottomed vessel and add the dry red chillies. Fry until they are almost black in colour, then add the onions. Sauté until translucent. Add the ginger paste and stir fry for a minute. Add the red chilli, turmeric and coriander powders and salt.

◆ Add the meat and *bhunao* (see p. 21) it with the garlic water until the water is absorbed. The meat should be brown in colour.

◆ Add the coconut milk to ½ a cup of warm water and cook on low heat until the meat becomes tender and the gravy, thick.

◆ Add the black peppercorn powder and the lemon juice. Stir and heat thoroughly.

Gosht Lazeez ▶

BHUTE MAHSOO

(Boneless meat with an assortment of spices)

Serves: 4

INGREDIENTS

500 gm	Lamb / mutton, boneless, without fat, cut into small cubes
100 ml / ½ cup	Mustard oil *(sarson ka tel)*
9 gm / 1½ tsp	Ginger *(adrak)* paste
9 gm / 1½ tsp	Garlic *(lasan)* paste
150 gm / ½ cup	Onion *(piyaz)* paste
5	Cloves *(laung)*
5	Green cardamoms *(elaichi)*, cracked
1	Cinnamon *(dalchini)* stick, 1"
2	Black cardamom seeds *(bari elaichi)*, crushed
1 ½ gm / 1 tsp	Anise pepper *(chakri phool)* powder
10	Peppercorns *(kali mirch)*
4½ gm / 3 tsp	Red chilli *(lal mirch)* powder
	Salt to taste

METHOD

◆ Heat the mustard oil in the frying pan until it smokes. Add the ginger, garlic and onion pastes and sauté until golden brown in colour. Reduce heat and add the cloves, green caradamoms, cinnamon and black cardamom seeds. Stir until they crackle.

◆ Add the lamb / mutton and cook for 10 minutes, stirring constantly, until the water has evaporated. Fry until brown in colour; add anise pepper powder, peppercorns, red chilli powder and salt to taste. Stir well; add 1 cup of water and simmer until the meat is tender and little or no water remains.

ROGHAN JOSH

(An aromatic lamb / mutton dish)

Serves: 6

INGREDIENTS

750 gm	Lamb / mutton, cut into pieces
200 ml / 1 cup	Yoghurt *(dahi)*
1 gm / ½ tsp	Asafoetida *(hing)*, dissolved in 2 tbsp of water
1 gm / ½ tsp	Red chilli *(lal mirch)* powder
100 ml / ½ cup	Clarified butter *(ghee)* / refined oil
180 gm / ¾ cup	Onions *(piyaz)*, finely chopped
2 gm / 1½ tsp	Turmeric *(haldi)* powder

Make the spice paste in a blender with a little water:

12 gm / 2 tsp	Ginger *(adrak)* paste
12 gm / 2 tsp	Garlic *(lasan)* paste
3 gm / 1½ tsp	Poppy seeds *(khus khus)*
2 gm / 1½ tsp	Cumin seeds *(jeera)*
8 gm / 4 tsp	Coriander seeds *(dhaniya)*
6	Cloves *(laung)*
8	Cardamom seeds *(elaichi)*
12	Peppercorns *(kali mirch)*
6	Almonds *(badam)*, blanched, peeled
	Salt to taste
2 gm / 1 tsp	Garam masala (fragrant, see p. 18)

METHOD

◆ Marinate the meat in the yoghurt, asafoetida and red chilli powder. Mix well and keep aside for 30 minutes.
◆ Heat the clarified butter / oil in a pan; when hot, add the onions. Sauté till the onions turn golden brown. Add the turmeric and the spice paste. Reduce heat and *bhunao* (see p. 21) for 8 minutes. Do not let the mixture become too dry.
◆ Increase the heat and add the meat with the marinade and salt. Cook until the water evaporates, stirring to get an even colour. Add water, reduce heat and cover the pan. Cook on very low heat till the meat is tender. Add the garam masala and stir till well mixed.

Roghan Josh ▶

MIRCHI ROGHAN JOSH

(Chilli lamb / mutton)

Serves: 4

INGREDIENTS

500 gm	Lamb / mutton, cut into pieces
8	Red chillies *(lal mirch)*, whole, dry and deseeded
100 ml / ½ cup	Clarified butter *(ghee)* / refined oil
100 ml / ½ cup	Yoghurt *(dahi)*, whisked
4	Green cardamoms *(elaichi)*, cracked
4	Cloves *(laung)*
3 gm / 2 tsp	Aniseed *(saunf)* powder
2 gm / 1½ tsp	Cinnamon *(dalchini)* powder
1 gm / ½ tsp	Black cumin seeds *(kala jeera)*
2 gm / 1 tsp	Dry ginger powder *(sonth)*
	Salt to taste
1 tsp	Red food colour, dissolved in ½ cup of water

METHOD

◆ Soak the red chillies in 1 cup of water for 2 hours; then make a paste with a little water. Pass the paste through a fine sieve into a bowl.
◆ Heat the clarified butter / oil in an earthen pot; add the yoghurt and fry until brown in colour. Put in the meat with the green cardamoms and cloves and stir fry until the meat is evenly coloured.
◆ Add the aniseed powder, cinnamon powder, black cumin seeds, dry ginger powder and salt. Add the sieved red chilli paste and water to the meat. Stir. Add the dissolved red colour. Stir and bring to a boil. Reduce heat and cook until the meat becomes tender. Simmer, stirring occasionally, until the clarified butter / oil comes to the surface.

KEBABI KOFTA

(Kebab-style kofta curry)

Serves: 4

INGREDIENTS

500 gm	Lamb / mutton, finely minced
	Salt to taste
6 gm / 4 tsp	Red chilli *(lal mirch)* powder
100 gm / 4 tbsp	Onion *(piyaz)*, fried and ground to a paste
9 gm / 3 tsp	Cumin seed *(jeera)* powder
8 gm / 4 tsp	Garam masala (standard, see p. 18)
12 gm / 2 tsp	Ginger *(adrak)* paste
12 gm / 4	Green chillies *(hari mirch)*, finely chopped
4 gm / 1 tbsp	Coriander leaves *(hara dhaniya)*, finely chopped
100 ml / ½ cup	Clarified butter *(ghee)* / refined oil
4	Bayleaves *(tejpatta)*
400 ml / 2 cups	Yoghurt *(dahi)*, thick
6 gm / 4 tsp	Red chilli *(lal mirch)* powder

For smoking the mince:

2 gm / 1 tsp	Cumin seeds *(jeera)*

METHOD

◆ Marinate the mince with salt, red chilli powder, half the onion paste, cumin seed powder, garam masala, ginger paste, green chillies and coriander leaves. Knead well while mixing. Keep aside for half an hour.

◆ Smoke the mince. Use the method as stated under *dhungar* (see p. 20).

◆ Wetting your hands, make koftas in the shape of sausages. The length of each should be at least 4-5 inches as they will shrink when cooked. Lay them out in a greased tray. Keep aside.

◆ Heat the clarified butter / oil in a large, deep pan. Add the bayleaves and fry for 1 minute. Remove the pan from the heat and let it cool. Very carefully, add 4 cups of water and put the pan back on the heat, bringing the water to a boil. Add the koftas one at a time. Boil uncovered, until they are firm. Reduce heat, cover and cook for 10-12 minutes.

◆ Add the yoghurt, red chilli powder and the remainder of the onion paste. Reduce the heat and simmer until the gravy becomes thick and the clarified butter / oil rises to the surface.

Kebabi Kofta ▶

LACHHEDAR GOSHT

(Crispy shredded meat)

Serves: 6-8

INGREDIENTS

1 kg	Lamb / mutton, large boneless pieces
100 ml / ½ cup	Clarified butter *(ghee)* / refined oil
9 gm / 6 tsp	Red chilli *(lal mirch)* powder
9 gm / 3 tsp	Cumin seed *(jeera)* powder
3 gm / ½ tbsp	Cardamom seed *(elaichi)* powder
4 gm / 2 tsp	Dry mango powder *(amchur)*
½ gm / ½ tsp	Saffron *(kesar)* soaked in 4 tbsp hot water
	Salt to taste

METHOD

◆ Boil the lamb / mutton in water, long enough so that the water dries when the meat becomes tender. Remove and shred the meat into thin, long pieces.

◆ Heat clarified butter / oil and fry the shredded meat on very low heat until crisp. Add all the ingredients and heat thoroughly. Mix well and serve.

SAFED RAJASTHANI MAANS

(White Rajasthani meat)

Serves: 4

INGREDIENTS

500 gm	Lamb / mutton, cubed
100 ml / ½ cup	Clarified butter *(ghee)* / refined oil
45 ml / 3 tbsp	Yoghurt *(dahi)*
3 gm / 2 tsp	Red chilli *(lal mirch)* seeds, dry, ground
9 gm / 1 ½ tsp	Ginger *(adrak)* paste
10	Almonds *(badam)*, blanched, peeled and ground with water
12 gm / 6 tsp	Poppy seeds *(khus khus)*, ground with water
9 gm / 6 tsp	Coconut *(nariyal)*, grated and ground
12½ gm / 2½ tbsp	Wholemilk fudge *(khoya)*
120 ml	Milk
15 ml / 1 tbsp	Vetivier *(kewra)* essence
30 ml / 2 tbsp	Lemon *(nimbu)* juice
1 ½ gm / 1 tsp	Aniseed *(saunf)* powder
	Salt to taste

METHOD

◆ Boil the lamb / mutton in plenty of water for 5 minutes. This will remove the colour from the meat. Discard the water and wash the meat under running water. Keep aside.

◆ In a bowl mix the meat with the yoghurt, salt, ground seeds of the red chillies and ginger paste.

◆ Heat the clarified butter / oil in an earthen pot, then add the meat. Stir until well mixed. Add only that much water which dries when the meat becomes tender.

◆ Add the almond and poppy seed pastes, ground coconut, *khoya* and milk. Mix well and simmer until the clarified butter / oil surfaces. Add the vetivier essence, lemon juice and aniseed powder. Heat thoroughly.

Safed Rajasthani Maans ▶

MAMSAM CHETTINAD

(Aromatic Tamil Nadu lamb / mutton curry)

Serves: 4

INGREDIENTS

500 gm	Lamb / mutton, boneless, cut into small cubes
150 ml / ¾ cup	Clarified butter *(ghee)* / refined oil
3	Black cardamoms *(bari elaichi)*, cracked
3	Green cardamoms *(elaichi)*, cracked
3	Cloves *(laung)*
2	Cinnamon *(dalchini)*, sticks, 1"
180 gm / ¾ cup	Onions *(piyaz)*, finely chopped
3	Red chillies *(lal mirch)*, dry, crushed
12	Peppercorns *(kali mirch)*, coarsely ground
8	Curry leaves *(meethi neem ke patte)*
⅓	Coconut *(nariyal)*, ground
1	Lemon *(nimbu)*, juice

METHOD

◆ Heat the clarified butter *(ghee)* / oil in a deep frying pan. When hot add the black and green cardamoms, cloves and cinnamon sticks. Fry until aromatic. Add the onions and sauté until translucent.

◆ Add the meat with the dry red chillies, peppercorns and curry leaves. Fry until the meat is lightly browned. Add 1 cup of water and cook on low heat until the meat becomes tender and very little water remains.

◆ Remove the pan from the heat. Add the ground coconut and the lime juice. Return to the fire and heat thoroughly until the dish has a thick gravy.

KEEMA LAL MIRCH

(Red peppers stuffed with mince)

Serves: 6-8

L A M B

72

INGREDIENTS

1 kg	Lamb / mutton, minced
12	Red capsicums / Peppers *(pahari mirch)* / Red pickle chillies *(sabut lal mirch)*
200 ml / 1 cup	Clarified butter *(ghee)* / refined oil
3	Onions *(piyaz),* finely chopped
1 ½ inch	Ginger *(adrak),* finely chopped
12	Garlic *(lasan)* cloves, finely chopped
100 ml / ½ cup	Hot water
4 gm / 2 tsp	Garam masala (see p. 18)
3 gm / 2 tsp	Anise pepper *(chakri phool)* powder
1½ gm / 1 tsp	Red chilli *(lal mirch)* powder
3 gm / 2 tsp	Coriander seed *(dhaniya)* powder
	Salt to taste

METHOD

◆ Cut around the stems of the red capsicums / red pickle chillies and scoop out the seeds and the pods. The openings should be such that they can later be stuffed with the cooked mince meat. Discard the seeds and the pods.

◆ Heat the clarified butter / oil and add the onions; sauté until translucent. Add the ginger and garlic. Sauté until they are brown in colour. Add water; bring to a boil and add the garam masala, anise pepper powder, red chilli powder and the coriander seed powder. Stir for 30 seconds, then add the mince meat and salt. Cook until the water evaporates. Add 1 ½ cups of water and cook until the meat is tender. Remove the dish from the heat and let it cool.

◆ Once the meat has cooled down, using a small spoon, stuff the capsicums / red chillies with the mince and put them back in the pan. Carefully cover the capsicums / chillies with the remainder of the mince and return to heat. Sprinkle ½ a cup of water and cook covered, stirring regularly until the capsicums / chillies are cooked and soft.

Keema Lal Mirch ▶

KEEMA AKBARI

(Almond and cashewnut mince meat)

Serves: 6

INGREDIENTS

750 gm	Lamb / mutton, minced
100 ml / ½ cup	Clarified butter *(ghee)* / refined oil
120 gm / ½ cup	Onions *(piyaz),* minced
12 gm / 1 tbsp	Garlic *(lasan),* chopped
200 ml / 1 cup	Yoghurt *(dahi),* whisked
2 gm / 1 tsp	Green cardamom seed *(elaichi)* powder
2 gm / 1 tsp	Peppercorn *(kali mirch)* powder
12 gm / 4	Green chillies *(hari mirch),* sliced
	Salt to taste

Make a paste with a little water:

15	Almonds *(badam),* blanched and peeled
12	Cashewnuts *(kaju)*
3 tsp	Poppy seeds *(khus khus),* roasted

METHOD

◆ Heat the clarified butter / oil in a pan and sauté the onions and chopped garlic on a low flame. Cook until translucent. Add the mince. Stir and cook on low heat until completely dry.

◆ Add the yoghurt with the cardamom powder, peppercorn powder, green chillies and salt. Simmer until the yoghurt is completely absorbed and the mince becomes tender.

◆ Add the almond-cashewnut-poppy seed paste and stir. Simmer on very low heat for 3 minutes, stirring all the time, being very careful that the paste does not burn.

GOSHT FALAKNUMA

(Masala meat)

Serves: 4

INGREDIENTS

500 gm	Lamb / mutton, cubed and boneless
100 ml / ½ cup	Clarified butter (ghee) / refined oil
12 gm / 2 tsp	Ginger (adrak) paste
12 gm / 2 tsp	Garlic (lasan) paste
	Salt to taste

For the masala:

75 gm / ¾ cup	Onions (piyaz), sliced
1 ½ gm / 1 tsp	Red chilli (lal mirch) powder
4 gm / 2 tsp	Garam masala (fragrant, see p. 18)
15 ml / 1 tbsp	Treacle or brown sugar, dissolved in 2 tbsp water
15 gm / 5	Green chillies (hari mirch), thinly sliced
20 gm / 25	Almonds (badam), blanched, peeled and ground to a paste
600 ml / 3 cups	Yoghurt (dahi), hung in a muslin cloth for at least 2 hours and then whisked
4 gm / 1 tbsp	Coriander leaves (hara dhaniya), fresh, chopped
½ gm / ½ tsp	Saffron (kesar), dissolved in 4 tbsp of hot water

METHOD

◆ Heat half the clarified butter / oil; add the ginger and garlic pastes and cook until golden in colour. Add the lamb / mutton and salt. Stir and add just enough water which will dry when the meat becomes tender.

◆ **For the masala,** in a frying pan, heat the balance of the clarified butter / oil. Add the onions and sauté until golden in colour. Add the red chilli powder, garam masala, treacle water, green chillies and the almond paste. Add ½ a cup of water and cook until the water dries up completely.

◆ Reheat the cooked meat and add the masala to it. Stir, add the yoghurt and the fresh coriander leaves. Mix well, add the saffron and simmer until the oil comes to the surface.

Gosht Falaknuma ▶

NALLI DUMPUKTH

(Lamb / mutton cooked in the sealed-pot style)

Serves: 6

INGREDIENTS

10	Lamb / mutton shanks
150 ml / ¾ cup	Clarified butter (ghee) / refined oil
6	Green cardamoms (elaichi), cracked
4	Cloves (laung)
45 gm / 2½ tbsp	Ginger (adrak) paste
55 gm / 3 tbsp	Garlic (lasan) paste
	Salt to taste
210 ml / 14 tbsp	Yoghurt (dahi)
60 gm / 3 tbsp	Onion (piyaz) paste, fried
2 gm / 1½ tsp	Red chilli (lal mirch) powder
600 ml / 3 cups	Meat stock
150 ml / ¾ cup	Tomato (tamatar) purée
15 gm / 1½ tbsp	Cashewnut (kaju) paste
2 gm / 1 tsp	Garam masala (standard, see p. 18)
12 gm / 1½ tsp	Ginger (adrak), juliennes
½ gm / ½ tsp	Saffron (kesar), soaked in 3 tbsp of warm milk

METHOD

◆ Heat the clarified butter / oil in a saucepan; when hot, add cardamoms and cloves. Fry until they crackle; fry ginger and garlic pastes till the water evaporates.

◆ Add the shanks with the salt, yoghurt, fried onion paste and red chilli powder. Mixing well, cook for 5 minutes. Add the meat stock; boil and simmer until the meat is tender. Remove the cooked meat from the gravy and place in an oven-proof casserole dish evenly.

◆ Sieve the gravy into another pan. Add the tomato purée, return the pan to heat. Stir and cook until the gravy is reduced, add the cashewnut paste and garam masala. Cook for 2 to 3 minutes. Pour the gravy over the meat and mix the ginger and saffron milk.

◆ Seal the casserole dish tightly with dough; bake in a preheated oven (177 °C / 350 °F) for 15-20 minutes. Remove and mix well.

KALEGI MASALA

(Sliced liver)

Serves: 4

INGREDIENTS

500 gm	Liver *(kalegi)*, sliced
12 gm / 2 tsp	Garlic *(lasan)* paste
12 gm / 2 tsp	Ginger *(adrak)* paste
1	Cinnamon *(dalchini)* stick, 2"

Grind together for a paste:

12 gm / 4	Green chillies *(hari mirch)*
8	Peppercorns *(kali mirch)*
2 gm / 1 tsp	Cumin seeds *(jeera)*
100 ml / ½ cup	Malt vinegar *(sirka)*
½ tsp	Sugar
100 ml / ½ cup	Clarified butter *(ghee)* / refined oil
180 gm / 1½ cups	Onions *(piyaz)*, finely sliced
	Salt to taste
2	Tomatoes *(tamatar)*, large, finely chopped

METHOD

◆ Boil the liver slices with the garlic and ginger pastes and cinnamon for 10 minutes, removing the scum. Remove the liver slices, wash and keep aside. Collect the stock for later use.
◆ Mix the ground paste into the liver slices and keep aside for half an hour.
◆ Heat the clarified butter / oil and sauté the onions until they are golden brown. Add the salt, the liver slices with the marinade and the stock. Bring to a boil and add the chopped tomatoes. Cook until all the water dries up.

Kalegi Masala ▶

KHASTA KALEGI

(Fried masala liver)

Serves: 6

INGREDIENTS

750 gm	Liver *(kalegi)*, thinly sliced

Marinate the liver well in the following and keep aside for 1 hour:

15 gm / 2½ tsp	Ginger *(adrak)* paste
15 gm / 2½ tsp	Garlic *(lasan)* paste
9 gm / 2 tsp	Salt
4 gm / 2½ tsp	Red chilli *(lal mirch)* powder
3 gm / 1½ tsp	Peppercorn *(kali mirch)* powder
1	Lemon *(nimbu)*, juice
100 ml / ½ cup	Clarified butter *(ghee)* / refined oil

METHOD

◆ In a large frying pan, heat the clarified butter / oil. When very hot, add the liver slices a few at a time. Fry until all the slices are crisp and tender. Remove with a slotted spoon and keep aside on a warmed serving dish. Serve immediately.

ANDE DUM KE

(Baked masala eggs)

Serves: 4

INGREDIENTS

6	Eggs *(ande)*, hard boiled, peeled and cut in half
100 ml / ½ cup	Clarified butter *(ghee)* / refined oil
3	Onions *(piyaz)*, medium-sized, ground to a paste with a little water
12 gm / 2 tsp	Ginger *(adrak)* paste
12 gm / 2 tsp	Garlic *(lasan)* paste
100 ml / ½ cup	Tomato *(tamatar)* purée
30 ml / 2 tbsp	Yoghurt *(dahi)*, whisked
1½ gm / 1 tsp	Turmeric *(haldi)* powder
3 gm / 1 tsp	Cumin seed *(jeera)* powder
1½ gm / 1 tsp	Coriander seed *(dhaniya)* powder
2 gm / 1½ tsp	Red chilli *(lal mirch)* powder
1½ gm / 1 tbsp	Dry fenugreek leaves *(kasoori methi)*
	Salt to taste

METHOD

◆ Place the egg halves in an oven-proof dish. They should not overlap.
◆ Heat the clarified butter / oil in a pan; add the onions and ginger and garlic pastes. Fry until brown. Add the tomato purée and yoghurt and cook until well blended. Then add the turmeric, cumin seeds, coriander seeds, and red chilli powders, the dry fenugreek leaves and salt. Stir for 1 minute. Add one cup of water and cook until the gravy becomes thick and well blended.
◆ Pour the gravy over the eggs, covering them completely. Cover the dish with foil and place it in an oven preheated to 180⁰ C / 356⁰ F. Remove after 10 minutes.

Ande Dum Ke ▶

MASALA GURDA

(Deep-fried kidneys)

Serves: 4

INGREDIENTS

500 gm	Kidneys *(gurda)*, skinned and cut in half down the centre
100 ml / ½ cup	Clarified butter *(ghee)* / refined oil
120 gm / 1 cup	Onions *(piyaz)*, sliced
25 gm / 2 tbsp	Ginger *(adrak)* paste
25 gm / 2 tbsp	Garlic *(lasan)* paste
18 gm / 6	Green chillies *(hari mirch)*, finely chopped
½ cup	Tomatoes *(tamatar)*, finely chopped
100 ml / ½ cup	Yoghurt *(dahi)*
4½ gm / 1½ tsp	Cumin seed *(jeera)* powder
2 gm / 1 ½ tsp	Coriander seed *(dhaniya)* powder
2 gm / 1½ tsp	Red chilli *(lal mirch)* powder
1 ½ gm / 1 tsp	Turmeric *(haldi)* powder
	Salt to taste
3 gm / 1½ tsp	Garam masala (standard, see p. 18)

METHOD

◆ Put the kidneys in a pan and add just enough water to cover them. Bring to a boil and remove the scum. Remove the pan from the heat; drain the water and wash the kidneys under running water. Repeat this process until no further scum rises. Drain and wash the kidneys under cold running water and keep aside.
◆ Heat the clarified butter / oil in a deep cooking pan. Add the onions and fry until translucent. Add the ginger and garlic pastes. Fry until golden brown in colour. Add the green chillies and chopped tomatoes and fry until well blended. Reduce the heat and add the yoghurt. Cook until the water evaporates. Add the cumin seed powder, coriander seed powder, red chilli powder, turmeric and salt. Mix well, cooking until the oil comes to the surface.
◆ Add the kidneys and garam masala with 1 cup of hot water. Bring to a boil and simmer until the water is reduced by three-fourths. Stir ocassionally. The gravy must be of a thick consistency.

OTHERS

GOAN MACHHI KARI

(Goan fish curry)

Serves: 6-8

INGREDIENTS

1 kg	Fish *(machhi)* steaks

Marinate the fish steaks in the following and keep aside:

1	Lemon *(nimbu)*, juice
3 gm / ¾ tsp	Salt
1 ½ gm / ¾ tsp	Peppercorn *(kali mirch)* powder

For the spice paste:

11 gm / 2½ tbsp	Coconut *(nariyal)*, finely grated
6 gm / 1½ tbsp	Coriander seeds *(dhaniya)*
4 ½ gm / 2½ tsp	Cumin seeds *(jeera)*
1½ gm / ½ tsp	Fenugreek seeds *(methi dana)*
6	Cloves *(laung)*
8	Red chillies *(lal mirch)*, dried, soaked in hot water for 15 minutes
24 gm / 6 tsp	Garlic *(lasan)*, chopped
12 gm / 1½ tsp	Ginger *(adrak)*, chopped
60 ml / 4 tbsp	Refined oil / coconut *(nariyal)* oil
180 gm / ¾ cup	Onions *(piyaz)*, chopped
400 ml / 2 cups	Coconut milk *(nariyal ka doodh)*
2 tbsp	Tamarind *(imli)*, pulp
	Salt to taste

METHOD

◆ Dry roast the coconut, coriander seeds, cumin seeds, fenugreek seeds and cloves separately until they turn brown in colour. Cool and make a paste in a blender with the soaked red chillies, garlic and ginger, adding a little water to make the paste smooth.

◆ Heat the oil in a deep frying pan; when hot, add the onions. Fry until soft. Add the spice paste and fry until it darkens. Add the coconut milk, tamarind pulp and salt. Lower the heat and simmer slowly, stirring all the time.

◆ Add the fish steaks with the marinade and stir slowly. Bring to a slow boil and simmer uncovered until the fish is cooked.

Goan Machhi Kari ▶

MACHLI KA SALAN

(Fish fillet treat)

Serves: 8-10

INGREDIENTS

1 ½ kg	Fish *(machhi)* fillets, round

Mix together and marinate the fish for 30 minutes:

3 gm / 2 tsp	Red chilli *(lal mirch)* powder
12 gm / 2 tsp	Green chilli *(hari mirch)* paste
12 gm / 2 tsp	Garlic *(lasan)* paste
12 gm / 2 tsp	Ginger *(adrak)* paste
12 gm / 3 tbsp	Mint leaves *(pudina)* paste
4 ½ gm / 3 tsp	Coriander seed *(dhaniya)* powder
1 ½ gm / 1 tsp	Turmeric *(haldi)* powder
175 ml / ¾ cup	Clarified butter *(ghee)* / refined oil
300 gm / 1½ cups	Onions *(piyaz)*, chopped
	Salt to taste

METHOD

◆ Heat the clarified butter / oil in a large frying pan and add the chopped onions. Sauté until light brown in colour.

◆ Add the marinated fish fillets. Reduce the heat and add ½ a cup of warm water and salt. Cook, stirring carefully, taking care the fish pieces do not break. Cook until the fish is tender and the gravy is thick.

MACHHI PAHALGAMI

(Tender fish slices cooked in yoghurt)

Serves: 6-8

INGREDIENTS

1 kg	White fish *(safed machhi)*, cut into firm, large slices
1 gm / ½ tsp	Turmeric *(haldi)* powder
3 gm / 2 tsp	Aniseed *(saunf)* powder
3 gm / 1½ tsp	Dry ginger powder *(sonth)*
200 ml / 1 cup	Clarified butter *(ghee)* / refined oil
12 gm / 2 tsp	Ginger *(adrak)* paste
6	Red chillies *(lal mirch)*, dry
3 gm / 2 tsp	Cumin seeds *(jeera)*
3 gm / 2 tsp	Coriander seed *(dhaniya)* powder
3 gm / 2 tsp	Red chilli *(lal mirch)* powder
350 ml / 1¾ cups	Yoghurt *(dahi)*, whisked
	Salt to taste

METHOD

◆ Marinate the fish pieces in the turmeric, aniseed and dry ginger powder for 1 hour.
◆ Heat the clarified butter / oil in a wok *(kadhai)* and fry the fish, one piece at a time. Fry until the pieces change colour. *(Do not overcook.)* Remove with a slotted spoon and keep aside on absorbent paper.
◆ In the same clarified butter / oil add the ginger paste, dry red chillies, cumin seeds, coriander seed powder and red chilli powder. Fry for 1 minute.
◆ Reduce heat and add the yoghurt and cook until the clarified butter / oil separates from the masala. Add the fish slices and salt. Stir and simmer, keeping the wok covered, until the fish is well coated with the masala, and becomes tender.

Machhi Pahalgami ▶

MACHLI TAMATAR KA SALAN

(Tomato fish curry)

Serves: 6-8

INGREDIENTS

1 kg	Fish *(machhi)* pieces, 1" x 2" each
1 ½ gm / 1 tsp	Turmeric *(haldi)* powder
	Salt to taste
100 ml / ½ cup	Clarified butter *(ghee)* / refined oil
240 gm / 1 cup	Onions *(piyaz)*, chopped
18 gm / 3 tsp	Garlic *(lasan)* paste
18 gm / 3 tsp	Ginger *(adrak)* paste
3 gm / 2 tsp	Red chilli *(lal mirch)* powder
2 gm / 1 tsp	Peppercorn *(kali mirch)* powder
2	Tomatoes *(tamatar)*, large, chopped coarsely

METHOD

◆ Dry the fish pieces; rub in the salt and turmeric and keep aside for half an hour.
◆ Heat the clarified butter / oil in a large saucepan. When hot, add the onions. Sauté until translucent. Add the garlic and ginger pastes, red chilli powder and peppercorn powder. Fry until light brown in colour.
◆ Add the fish pieces and stir gently for 2 to 3 minutes. Add the chopped tomatoes. Reduce heat and cook uncovered until the tomatoes are cooked and form a coarse pulp. Cook until the fish is tender and the gravy is thick.

NARIYAL MACHHI

(Coconut fish)

Serves: 6-8

INGREDIENTS

1 kg	White fish *(safed machhi)* fillets, cut into cubes firmly
For the marinade:	
3 gm / 2 tsp	Turmeric *(haldi)* powder
9 gm / 2 tsp	Salt
For the curry:	
100 ml / ½ cup	Mustard oil *(sarson ka tel)*
25 gm / 2 tbsp	Garlic *(lasan)*, finely chopped
6 gm / 2 tsp	Cumin seed *(jeera)* powder
3 gm / 2 tsp	Turmeric *(haldi)* powder
	Salt to taste
1 ½ gm / 1 tsp	Red chilli *(lal mirch)* powder
20	Curry leaves *(meethi neem ke patte)*
200 ml / 1 cup	Coconut milk *(nariyal ka doodh)*, thick, from 1 whole grated coconut
50 gm	Tamarind *(imli)* pulp, boiled in 2 cups of water and then sieved
45 gm / 15	Green chillies *(hari mirch)*, deseeded

METHOD

◆ Rub the turmeric powder and salt into the fish thoroughly. Keep aside for half an hour.

◆ Heat the mustard oil until it smokes. Fry the marinated fish cubes, two at a time, until they are golden in colour. Remove with a slotted spoon on to an absorbent sheet of paper. In the same oil, add the garlic and cook until it is light brown. Add the cumin seed powder, turmeric powder, salt, red chilli powder, curry leaves, coconut milk and the tamarind juice and green chillies. Stir rapidly and bring to a boil. Add the fried fish cubes and cook for 5 minutes.

Nariyal Machhi ▶

DOHI MAACH

(Deep-fried fish flavoured with raisins)

Serves: 6-8

INGREDIENTS

1 kg	White fish *(safed machhi)*, cut into cubes of 1" x 1½ "
Grind to a paste with a little water:	
180 gm / ¾ cup	Onions *(piyaz)*, chopped
25 gm / 3 tsp	Ginger *(adrak)*, chopped
8	Garlic *(lasan)* cloves
4½ gm / 1½ tsp	Cumin seed *(jeera)* powder
4 gm / 2 ½ tsp	Red chilli *(lal mirch)* powder
1 gm / ½ tsp	Turmeric *(haldi)* powder
100 ml / ½ cup	Mustard oil *(sarson ka tel)*
10	Sultanas *(kishmish)*, soaked in water for 10 minutes and sliced
200 ml / 1 cup	Yoghurt *(dahi)*, whisked
	Salt to taste

METHOD

◆ Apply the ground paste to the fish and keep aside for half an hour.

◆ Heat the mustard oil in a wok *(kadhai)* until the oil smokes. Remove the wok from the heat and cool the oil. Return to the heat and fry the fish pieces. When evenly golden in colour, add 4 tablespoons of water, the sultanas, the yoghurt and salt. Stir and simmer until all the liquid dries up and the fish is tender.

JHINGA JALFREZI

(Prawns garnished with coriander leaves)

Serves: 6

INGREDIENTS

750 gm	Prawns *(jhinga)*, deveined and washed
100 ml / ½ cup	Clarified butter *(ghee)* / refined oil
6	Red chillies *(lal mirch)*, dry, crushed
2 gm / 1 ½ tsp	Cumin seeds *(jeera)*
	Salt to taste
3 gm / 1 ½ tsp	Peppercorn *(kali mirch)* powder
16 gm / 2 tsp	Ginger *(adrak)* juliennes
100 ml / ½ cup	Tomato *(tamatar)* purée
22 ml / 1½ tbsp	White vinegar *(sirka)*
2 gm / ½ tbsp	Coriander leaves *(hara dhaniya)*, chopped

METHOD

◆ Heat the clarified butter / oil in a wok *(kadhai)*, and add the crushed, dry, red chillies. Stir and add the cumin seeds. When they crackle, add the prawns, salt, peppercorn powder and the ginger juliennes. Stir well. Cover the wok and reduce the heat. Cook on a slow fire until the prawns are almost tender.
◆ Add the tomato purée and white vinegar. Cook until the prawns become tender. Garnish with chopped coriander leaves.

Jhinga Jalfrezi ▶

PARSI JHINGA

(Parsi prawn curry)

Serves: 6-8

INGREDIENTS

500 gm	Prawns *(jhinga)*, shelled, deveined and washed
60 ml / 4 tbsp	Clarified butter *(ghee)* / refined oil
9 gm / 3 tsp	Mustard seeds *(sarson)*
6 gm / 2 tsp	Cumin seeds *(jeera)*
180 gm / ¾ cup	Onions *(piyaz)*, chopped finely
3 gm / ½ tsp	Garlic *(lasan)* paste
3 gm / ½ tsp	Ginger *(adrak)* paste
1 ½ gm / 1 tsp	Red chilli *(lal mirch)* powder
3	Green chillies *(hari mirch)*, chopped
1 ½ gm / 1 tsp	Turmeric *(haldi)* powder
1 ½ gm / 1 tsp	Coriander seed *(dhaniya)* powder
12 gm / 1 tbsp	Sugar
30 ml / 2 tbsp	Malt vinegar *(sirka)*
	Salt to taste

METHOD

◆ Heat the clarified butter / oil in a wok *(kadhai)*; add the mustard seeds and cumin seeds and when they crackle, add the onions. Sauté for 1 minute, add the garlic and ginger pastes, red chilli powder, green chillies, turmeric and coriander seed powders and sugar. Cook until the onions turn brown.
◆ Add the prawns and simmer until cooked.
◆ Add the malt vinegar and salt and cook until the prawns are well coated with the gravy.

JHINGA KARI

(Tangy prawn curry)

Serves: 4

INGREDIENTS

500 gm	Prawns *(jhinga)*, shelled, deveined
15 ml / 1 tbsp	Lemon *(nimbu)* juice
15 ml / 1 tbsp	Clarified butter *(ghee)* / refined oil
3	Tomatoes *(tamatar)*, quartered
10	Garlic *(lasan)* cloves
16 gm / 2 tsp	Ginger *(adrak)*, shredded
6	Green chillies *(hari mirch)*, slit lengthways
3 gm / 2 tsp	Red chilli *(lal mirch)* powder
1½ gm / 1 tsp	Turmeric *(haldi)* powder
3 gm / 1 tsp	Cumin seed *(jeera)* powder
	Salt to taste

METHOD

◆ Mix the prawns well with the lemon juice. Keep for 10 minutes. Wash under running water. Drain and keep aside.

◆ Heat the clarified butter / oil in a wok *(kadhai)* and add the tomatoes. Stir and add the garlic cloves, ginger and green chillies. Sauté until the tomatoes are soft, but not broken. Add ½ a cup of water, bring to a boil and add the red chilli powder, turmeric powder, cumin seed powder and salt. Mix well and add the prawns. Cook for 8 to 10 minutes until the water dries and the prawns are ready.

Jhinga Kari ▶

JHINGA BALCHAO

(Fried prawns laced with spices and condiments)

Serves: 6-8

INGREDIENTS

1 kg	Prawns *(jhinga)*, deveined and without their heads
200 ml / 1 cup	Clarified butter / refined oil for deep frying
For the masala:	
200 ml / 1 cup	Clarified butter *(ghee)* / refined oil
240 gm / 1 cup	Onions *(piyaz)*, chopped
½ cup	Tomatoes *(tamatar)*, chopped
For the paste, blend together:	
12 gm / 25	Red chillies *(lal mirch)*, dry
2	Cinnamon *(dalchini)* sticks
10	Green cardamoms *(elaichi)*
4	Black cardamoms *(bari elaichi)*
15	Cloves *(laung)*
1 tsp	Peppercorns *(kali mirch)*
2 gm / 1 tsp	Cumin seeds *(jeera)*
50 gm / 2 tbsp	Ginger *(adrak)*, chopped
150 ml / ¾ cup	Malt vinegar *(sirka)*
12	Curry leaves *(meethi neem ke patte)*
6 gm / 2 tsp	Sugar
	Salt to taste

METHOD

◆ Heat the oil and fry the prawns. Remove with a slotted spoon and keep on an absorbent paper.

◆ Heat 1 cup refined oil, add the onions and fry until golden brown. Add the tomatoes and stir for 2 minutes. Add the paste and fry until aromatic.

◆ Add the fried prawns and stir until cooked. Then add the curry leaves and sugar. Stir and add the salt. The balchao tastes best if left to mature for at least two days.

FISH

SONDHIA

(Princely prawns)

Serves: 6-8

INGREDIENTS

1 kg	Prawns *(jhinga)*, shelled, deveined, washed and dried with paper towels. (Wash and keep the shells.)
1	Cinnamon *(dalchini)* stick, 2"
20	Peppercorns *(kali mirch)*

Marinate the prawns in the following for 1 hour:

2 gm / 1 ½ tsp	Red chilli *(lal mirch)* powder
2 gm / 1 ½ tsp	Cumin seed *(jeera)*, roasted, powdered
3 gm / 2 tsp	Turmeric *(haldi)* powder
	Salt to taste
9 gm / 1½ tsp	Garlic *(lasan)* paste
4	Green chillies *(hari mirch)*, finely chopped
75 ml / 5 tbsp	Lemon *(nimbu)* juice
50 ml / ¼ cup	Clarified butter *(ghee)* / refined oil
12 gm / 3 tbsp	Coriander leaves *(hara dhaniya)*, finely chopped

METHOD

◆ Heat 1 ½ cups of water in a saucepan. Add the prawn shells, cinnamon stick and peppercorns and bring to a boil. Cover the pan and lower the heat. Simmer for 25 minutes. Strain the stock, discarding the shells and the whole spices. The stock should measure 1 cup.

◆ In a large frying pan, heat the clarified butter / oil and when hot, add the prawns with the marinade. Cook, stirring until the prawns turn pink in colour. Pour in the stock and bring to a rapid boil. Cook uncovered until the prawns are tender. *(Do not overcook the prawns and let them get too soft.)*

◆ Stir in the coriander leaves.

Sondhia ▶

METHI MAACH

(Fenugreek-flavoured fish)

Serves: 4

INGREDIENTS

500 gm	White fish *(machhi)*, firm and cut into 2" x 2" cubes
100 ml / ½ cup	Clarified butter *(ghee)* / refined oil
3 gm / 1 tsp	Fenugreek seeds *(methi dana)*
2	Red chillies *(lal mirch)*, dry
100 ml / ½ cup	Yoghurt *(dahi)*
4 ½ gm / 3 tsp	Red chilli *(lal mirch)* powder
4 ½ gm / 3 tsp	Coriander seed *(dhaniya)* powder
2 gm / 1½ tsp	Cumin seeds *(jeera)*
2 gm / 1½ tsp	Turmeric *(haldi)* powder
75 gm / 3 tbsp	Onion *(piyaz)* paste
18 gm / 3 tsp	Garlic *(lasan)* paste
9 gm / 1½ tsp	Ginger *(adrak)* paste
1 gm / 2 tsp	Dry fenugreek leaves *(kasoori methi)*
	Salt to taste

METHOD

◆ Wash the fish pieces and dry them thoroughly.

◆ Heat the clarified butter / oil; add the fenugreek seeds and dry red chillies. Fry until they turn black in colour. Remove from the refined oil and discard.

◆ Reduce the heat and add all the other ingredients and fry until well browned and the masala separates from the oil.

◆ Add the fish pieces and stir. Cook on low heat, stirring occasionally. Cook until the fish is tender and no liquid remains.

F I S H

ALU DUM

(Potatoes flavoured with ginger and yoghurt)

Serves: 4-6

INGREDIENTS

500 gm	Potatoes *(alu)*, small, new, scrubbed but not peeled
30 ml / 2 tbsp	Clarified butter *(ghee)* / refined oil
1	Cinnamon *(dalchini)* stick, 1"
3	Green cardamoms *(elaichi)*, cracked
2	Cloves *(laung)*
1 gm / ½ tsp	Turmeric *(haldi)* powder
1 gm / ½ tsp	Aniseed *(saunf)* powder
1 gm / ½ tsp	Dry ginger *(sonth)* powder

For the blended mixture:

150 gm / ½ cup	Onions *(piyaz)* paste
6 gm / 1 tsp	Garlic *(lasan)* paste
6 gm / 1 tsp	Ginger *(adrak)* paste
15 ml / 1 tbsp	Lemon *(nimbu)* juice
15 ml / 1 tbsp	Water
	Salt to taste
100 ml / ½ cup	Yoghurt *(dahi)*, whisked
1 gm / ½ tsp	Cumin seeds *(jeera)*, dry, roasted
1 gm / ½ tsp	Garam masala (fragrant, see p. 18)

METHOD

◆ Boil the potatoes in water in a covered pan for 5 minutes; drain immediately. Prick the potatoes lightly all over with a toothpick. Keep aside.

◆ Heat the clarified butter / oil; add the cinnamon, cardamoms and cloves. Fry until they are fragrant. Reduce the heat to low, then add the turmeric, aniseed and dry ginger powder. Stir for 15 seconds. Add the blended mixture and cook until it is brown in colour.

◆ Add the potatoes and ¼ cup of water. Stir and cover the pan tightly and cook on very low heat until the potatoes become tender.

◆ Combine the whisked yoghurt with the cumin seeds and garam masala. Serve the potatoes with the yoghurt mixture spooned over.

Alu Dum ▶

ALU POSTOE

(Potatoes flavoured with poppy seeds)

Serves: 4-6

INGREDIENTS

1 kg	Potatoes *(alu)*, peeled and quartered
¾ cup	Poppy seeds *(khus khus)*
6 gm / 12	Red chillies *(lal mirch)*, dry
100 ml / 1 cup	Clarified butter *(ghee)* / refined oil
	Salt to taste
2	Lemons *(nimbu)*, juice

METHOD

◆ Grind the poppy seeds and red chillies with a little water to make a fine paste.

◆ Heat the clarified butter / oil in a wok *(kadhai)*; when hot, add the potatoes and fry until golden brown all over. Remove and keep aside on absorbent paper.

◆ In the same clarified butter / oil, add the ground paste. Fry until golden in colour and the clarified butter / oil separates. Add the fried potatoes and salt. Stir and add ½ a cup of water. Cook until the water is completely absorbed. Add the lemon juice. Mix well.

VEGETABLES

92

ALU TAMATAR TARIWALA

(Potato-tomato curry)

Serves: 4

INGREDIENTS

5	Potatoes *(alu)*, medium-sized, peeled, cut into chunks and immersed in water
100 ml / ½ cup	Mustard oil *(sarson ka tel)*
3	Red chillies *(lal mirch)*, whole, dry
6 gm / 1 tbsp	Coriander *(dhaniya)* seeds
2 ½ gm / ½ tsp	Asafoetida *(hing)*
3 cups	Tomatoes *(tamatar)*, coarsely chopped
2 gm / 1 ½ tsp	Turmeric *(haldi)* powder
1 ½ gm / ¾ tsp	Red chilli *(lal mirch)* powder
	Salt to taste
18 gm / 6	Green chillies *(hari mirch)*, split, with the stems removed
12 ½ gm / ½ cup	Coriander leaves *(hara dhaniya)*, chopped

METHOD

◆ Heat the mustard oil till it smokes. Reduce the heat, add the red chillies and coriander seeds. When they crackle, add the asafoetida, stir and add the tomatoes. Cook for 1 minute; add the turmeric, red chilli powder and salt. Cook until the tomatoes become soft, pulpy and well blended.

◆ Add 1 ½ cups of water, bring to a boil and add the drained potatoes and green chillies. Cook until they become tender and there is a lot of curry.

◆ Garnish with coriander leaves.

Alu Tamatar Tariwala ▲

ALU KORMA

(Almond-flavoured potato curry)

Serves: 4-6

INGREDIENTS

500 gm	Potatoes *(alu)*, washed and quartered
100 ml / ½ cup	Yoghurt *(dahi)*

Dry roast and grind to a paste with a little water:

3 tbsp	Almonds *(badam)*, blanched, peeled and sliced
4 ½ gm / 3 tsp	Coconut *(nariyal)*, grated
6 gm / 3 tsp	Poppy seeds *(khus khus)*
6 gm / 3 tsp	Coriander seeds *(dhaniya)*
4 ½ gm / 3 tsp	Red chilli *(lal mirch)* powder
100 ml / ½ cup	Clarified butter *(ghee)* / refined oil
120 gm / ½ cup	Onions *(piyaz)*, chopped
12 gm / 2 tsp	Ginger *(adrak)* paste
12 gm / 2 tsp	Garlic *(lasan)* paste
	Salt to taste

METHOD

◆ Whisk the yoghurt with the roasted paste. Mix well.

◆ Heat the clarified butter / oil; reduce the heat, add onions, ginger and garlic pastes. Fry until golden brown.

◆ Add the potatoes and fry until golden brown. Add the yoghurt mixture and salt. Cook for 5 minutes and add ¾ cup of warm water. Bring to a boil, reduce heat and cook until the potatoes are tender and the gravy is thick.

Alu Korma ▶

SAAG ALU

(Peppy spinach and potatoes)

Serves: 4-6

INGREDIENTS

500 gm	Spinach *(palak)*, washed and cut
500 gm	Potatoes *(alu)*, diced
100 ml / ½ cup	Clarified butter *(ghee)* / refined oil
1	Onions *(piyaz)*, large, sliced
6 gm / 1 tsp	Ginger *(adrak)* paste
6 gm / 1 tsp	Garlic *(lasan)* paste
1 ½ gm / 1 tsp	Coriander seed *(dhaniya)* powder
1 ½ gm / 1 tsp	Red chilli *(lal mirch)* powder
2 gm / 1 tsp	Peppercorn *(kali mirch)* powder
	Salt to taste

METHOD

◆ Boil the spinach and potatoes for 10 minutes, with just enough water to cover them. Drain and keep aside.

◆ Heat the clarified butter / oil and add the onions and ginger and garlic pastes. Sauté for 2 minutes. Add the coriander powder, red chilli powder and peppercorn powder. Mix well and add the spinach and potatoes.

◆ Bring to a boil (the water should be released by the spinach), reduce heat and cook covered until the potatoes are tender. Add salt and stir.

VEGETABLES

SARSON KA SAAG

(Spicy green Punjab speciality)

Serves: 4-6

INGREDIENTS

1 kg	Mustard greens *(sarson)*, finely chopped
250 gm	Spinach *(palak)*, finely chopped
25 gm / 3 tbsp	Maize flour *(makkai ka atta)*, sieved at least 3 times
	Salt to taste
100 ml / ½ cup	Clarified butter *(ghee)* / refined oil
24 gm / 3 tsp	Ginger *(adrak)*, chopped
5	Garlic *(lasan)* cloves, chopped
3	Green chillies *(hari mirch)*, finely chopped
3	Red chillies *(lal mirch)*, whole

METHOD

◆ Boil the mustard greens and spinach until soft. Drain and blend to make a coarse paste. Keep aside.
◆ Heat a pan and add the green paste. Put in 1 cup of water. Cook, stirring and mashing the paste against the side of the pan. Add the maize flour and salt and cook for at least 45 minutes, adding water as and when required.
◆ Heat the clarified butter / oil in a frying pan; add the ginger, garlic and green chillies. Fry until they change colour. Add the whole red chillies. Fry for 2 minutes. Pour over the green paste and mix well. Cook for a further 30 minutes.

Sarson Ka Saag ▶

MAKKAI KI ROTI

(Maize bread)

Serves: 4

INGREDIENTS

1 ½ cups	Maize flour *(makkai ka atta)*
½ cup	Wheat flour *(gehu ka atta)*
4½ gm / 1 tsp	Salt
	Clarified butter *(ghee)* for frying

METHOD

◆ Sieve the maize, wheat flour and salt. Make a smooth dough with warm water and cover for 10 minutes with a wet cloth.
◆ Divide the dough into 8 equal parts and flatten each to form a disc. Sprinkle the disc with flour and carefully roll out to make a *roti* 5″ in diameter. Heat a griddle on medium heat and lay the *roti* flat onto it. Add a little clarified butter on the sides and fry. Turn the *roti* over and do the same till cooked.

SEM KE PHALI KA SALAN

(Beans flavoured with sesame seeds)

Serves: 4-6

INGREDIENTS

450 gm	Green beans *(sem)*, with the ends cut, string removed and cut into 2 pieces each
100 ml / ½ cup	Clarified butter *(ghee)* / refined oil
60 gm / ½ cup	Onions *(piyaz)*, finely sliced
6 gm / 1½ tbsp	Sesame seeds *(til)*, ground to a paste with a little water
3 gm / ½ tsp	Garlic *(lasan)* paste
3 gm / ½ tsp	Ginger *(adrak)* paste
3 gm / 2 tsp	Red chilli *(lal mirch)* powder / Salt to taste

METHOD

◆ Heat the clarified butter / oil in a pan; when hot, add the onions. Sauté till they are golden brown. Add the sesame seed paste, garlic and ginger pastes, red chilli powder and salt. Fry till golden in colour.
◆ Add the beans and fry till they change colour. Add ¾ cup of hot water and bring to a boil. Reduce heat, cover and cook till the beans become tender and the clarified butter / oil comes to the surface.

V E G E T A B L E S

BAIGAN NARIYAL

(Eggplants laced with coconut)

Serves: 4-6

INGREDIENTS

2	Eggplants *(baigan)*, big
100 ml / ½ cup	Clarified butter *(ghee)* / refined oil
4 ½ gm / 1 tbsp	Coconut *(nariyal)*, finely grated
90 gm / ¾ cup	Onions *(piyaz)*, sliced
4	Green chillies *(hari mirch)*, chopped
25 gm / 1 tbsp	Ginger *(adrak)*, minced
200 ml / 1 cup	Coconut *(nariyal)* milk, thick
	Salt to taste
45 ml / 3 tbsp	Vinegar *(sirka)*
1 ½ gm / 1 tsp	Red chilli *(lal mirch)* powder

METHOD

◆ Roast the eggplants all over, on an open flame or on a grill, until the skin turns black. Toss into chilled water. When cool, remove from the water and peel the skin. Remove the stem and scoop out the pulp and mash in a mixing bowl.

◆ Heat the clarified butter / oil in a wok *(kadhai)* and fry the grated coconut, onions, green chillies and ginger until golden brown. Add the mashed eggplant, coconut milk, salt, vinegar and red chilli powder. Cook until well blended and the oil rises to the surface.

Baigan Nariyal ▶

VEGETABLES

BHARTA

(Appetizing eggplants)

Serves: 4-6

INGREDIENTS

750 gm	Eggplants *(baigan)*
450 gm	Tomatoes *(tamatar)*, blanched, peeled and chopped
4 gm / 2 tsp	Coriander seed *(dhaniya)* powder
2 gm / 1 tsp	Cumin seed *(jeera)* powder
1 ½ gm / 1 tsp	Turmeric *(haldi)* powder
8 gm / 2 tbsp	Coriander leaves *(hara dhaniya)*, chopped
100 ml / ½ cup	Clarified butter *(ghee)* / refined oil
120 gm / ½ cup	Onions *(piyaz)*, chopped
4 gm / 1 tsp	Garlic *(lasan)*, chopped
12 gm / 1½ tsp	Ginger *(adrak)*, chopped
6 gm / 2	Green chillies *(hari mirch)*, chopped
½	Lemon *(nimbu)*, juice
	Salt to taste

METHOD

◆ Cut the eggplants into quarters. Lay them out in an oven-proof dish with the pulp-side up. Cover the dish with aluminium foil and bake in the oven preheated to 180⁰ C / 356⁰ F, for 1 hour. Remove the dish from the oven and scoop out the pulp from the eggplant with a spoon and place in a mixing bowl. Discard the skins.

◆ Add the tomatoes, coriander seed powder, cumin seed powder, turmeric powder and 1 tbsp coriander leaves to the pulp and mix well. Set aside.

◆ Heat the clarified butter / oil in a pan; when hot, add the onions and sauté until translucent. Add the garlic, ginger and chillies. Fry until the ginger and garlic turn golden in colour. Add the eggplant mixture with the salt. Cook, stirring frequently. Add the lemon juice, mix well and garnish with coriander leaves.

KHATHA~MEETHA BAIGAN

(Sweet-and-sour eggplants)

Serves: 4

INGREDIENTS

500 gm	Eggplants *(baigan)*, the long variety with stems, 8 pieces
100 ml / ½ cup	Mustard oil *(sarson ka tel)*
6	Red chillies *(lal mirch)*, dry
240 gm / 1 cup	Onions *(piyaz)*, chopped
60 gm / ½ cup	Garlic *(lasan)*, chopped
40 gm / ½ cup	Ginger *(adrak)*, chopped
1 cup	Tamarind *(imli)*, extract
200 ml / 1 cup	Brown sugar
4 ½ gm / 3 tsp	Red chilli *(lal mirch)* powder
	Salt to taste

METHOD

◆ Heat the mustard oil in a wok *(kadhai)* until it smokes. Reduce the heat and fry the eggplants and remove with a slotted spoon. Keep aside. In the same oil, fry the dry red chillies, stirring for 30 seconds. Add the onions, garlic and ginger. Cook until translucent. Add the tamarind extract and brown sugar. Stir and add the red chilli powder and salt.

◆ Stir until well mixed; then add the fried eggplants. Cook on very low heat for 10 minutes, stirring occasionally.

Khatha~Meetha Baigan ▶

VEGETABLES

METHI DAHI

(Fenugreek-flavoured curd)

Serves: 4

INGREDIENTS

30 gm / 2 cups	Fenugreek *(methi)* leaves, picked and cleaned
100 ml / ½ cup	Clarified butter *(ghee)* / refined oil
1 gm / ¼ tsp	Asafoetida *(hing)*, dissolved in 1 tsp of water
1 gm / ½ tsp	Turmeric *(haldi)* powder
1	Ginger *(adrak)*, thinly sliced, 1"
3	Green chillies *(hari mirch)*, finely chopped
	Salt to taste
100 ml / ½ cup	Yoghurt *(dahi)*, whisked
1 gm / ½ tsp	Garam Masala (fragrant, see p. 18)

METHOD

◆ Boil the fenugreek leaves in water for 5 to 7 minutes. Cool and drain the leaves and squeeze out the water. Grind them in a blender to a fine paste. Keep aside.

◆ Heat the clarified butter / oil in a wok *(kadhai)* with the asafoetida water. When it splutters, add the fenugreek paste. Stir for 7-8 minutes.

◆ Add the turmeric powder, ginger slices, chopped green chillies and salt. Stir in half a cup of warm water and cook on low heat till the fenugreek is tender. Add the whisked yoghurt and stir it in till it is well blended and the clarified butter / oil comes to the surface.

◆ Sprinkle the garam masala just before serving.

PANEER ACHAARI

(Cottage cheese pickled with condiments)

Serves: 6-8

INGREDIENTS

600 gm	Cottage cheese *(paneer,* see p. 24), cut into cubes of 1" x 1"
100 ml / ½ cup	Clarified butter *(ghee)* / refined oil
6 gm / 4 tsp	Aniseed *(saunf)*
6 gm / 2 tsp	Black mustard seeds *(sarson)*
3 gm / 1 tsp	Fenugreek seeds *(methi dana)*
1 gm / ½ tsp	Nigella seeds *(kalongi)*
3 gm / 2 tsp	Cumin seeds *(jeera)*
300 gm / 1½ cups	Onions *(piyaz),* chopped
24 gm / 8	Green chillies *(hari mirch),* chopped
3 gm / 2 tsp	Turmeric *(haldi)* powder
18 gm / 3 tsp	Garlic *(lasan)* paste
18 gm / 3 tsp	Ginger *(adrak)* paste
200 ml / 1 cup	Yoghurt *(dahi),* whisked
6 gm / 3 tsp	Dry mango powder *(amchur)*
3 gm / 2 tsp	Red chilli *(lal mirch)* powder
6 gm / 2 tsp	Sugar
	Salt to taste

METHOD

◆ Heat the clarified butter / oil in a wok *(kadhai);* when hot, add the aniseed, mustard seeds, fenugreek seeds, nigella seeds and cumin seeds. Fry until they crackle. Add the onions and green chillies. Cook until golden brown. Add the turmeric powder, garlic and ginger pastes. Fry for 1 minute.
◆ Reduce the heat, add the yoghurt with the dry mango powder, red chilli powder, sugar and salt. Cook until the yoghurt is completely absorbed and the clarified butter / oil comes to the surface.
◆ Add the cottage cheese with 1 cup of warm water. Increase the heat and cook until the gravy becomes thick and the clarified butter / oil comes to the surface.

Paneer Achaari ▶

METHI CHAMAN

(Cottage cheese with spinach and fenugreek)

Serves: 4-6

INGREDIENTS

50 gm	Fenugreek *(methi)* leaves
50 gm	Spinach *(palak)* leaves
250 gm	Cottage cheese *(paneer,* see p. 24)
100 ml / ½ cup	Clarified butter *(ghee)* / refined oil
2 ½ gm / ½ tsp	Asafoetida *(hing)*
2 gm / 1 tsp	Cumin seeds *(jeera)*
5	Cloves *(laung)*
1 ½ gm / 1 tsp	Turmeric *(haldi)* powder
1 ½ gm / 1 tsp	Red chilli *(lal mirch)* powder
8 gm / 1 tsp	Ginger *(adrak),* chopped
1 gm / ½ tsp	Dry ginger powder *(sonth)*
1 tsp	Coriander leaves *(hara dhaniya),* ground
6 gm / 2 tsp	Sugar
400 ml / 2 cups	Water
	Salt to taste

METHOD

◆ Clean the fenugreek and spinach leaves and grind them together to form a smooth paste.
◆ Cut the cottage cheese into 1" x 1" cubes and fry until golden brown. Drain and keep aside.
◆ Heat the clarified butter / oil in a wok *(kadhai);* add the asafoetida, cumin seeds and cloves. Fry until they crackle. Add the green paste. Lower heat until it is cooked. Add the turmeric powder, red chilli powder, ginger, dry ginger powder, ground coriander leaves, salt and sugar. Stir to mix well and add the water. Bring to a boil; then add the cottage cheese. Cook until the water evaporates.

SAUNFIA CHAMAN

(Aromatic cottage cheese curry)

Serves: 4

INGREDIENTS

350 gm	Cottage cheese *(paneer see p. 24)*
200 ml / 1 cup	Clarified butter *(ghee)* / refined oil
17½ ml / 3½ tsp	Clarified butter *(ghee)* / refined oil
2 gm / 1 tsp	Dry ginger powder *(sonth)*
1½ gm / 1 tsp	Aniseed *(saunf)* powder
1½ gm / 1 tsp	Cinnamon *(dalchini)* powder
3 gm / 2 tsp	Red chilli *(lal mirch)* powder
6	Green cardamom seeds *(elaichi),* powdered
	Salt to taste
100 gm / 4 tbsp	Onion *(piyaz)* paste, fried
½ tsp	Red edible colour diluted in 4 tbsp of water

METHOD

◆ Cut the cottage cheese into 1" x 1" cubes. Heat the clarified butter / oil for frying and fry the cottage cheese cubes until golden brown all over. Remove with a slotted spoon and immerse in a bowl of water. Keep for 15 minutes and drain. Discard the water and keep the cheese cubes aside.

◆ Heat the clarified butter / oil in a wok *(kadhai)*. Add the dry ginger powder, aniseed powder, cinnamon powder, red chilli powder, cardamom powder and salt. Stir and add two cups of water. Bring to a boil till the water is reduced by one-fourth. Then add the fried cottage cheese cubes, bring to a boil and add the onion paste. Simmer until the gravy becomes thick and the oil comes to the surface.

Saunfia Chaman ▲

GOBI CHAMAN

(Fried cottage cheese and cauliflower sprinkled with cumin seeds)

Serves: 4-6

INGREDIENTS

500 gm	Cottage cheese *(paneer,* see p. 24) cut into large, thin rectangles
500 gm	Cauliflower *(phool gobi),* washed and cut into large florets
150 ml / ¾ cup	Mustard oil *(sarson ka tel)*
50 ml / ¼ cup	Clarified butter *(ghee) /* refined oil
4 ½ gm / 1 tbsp	Aniseed *(saunf)* powder
1 gm / ½ tsp	Dry ginger *(sonth)* powder
1 gm / ½ tsp	Turmeric *(haldi)* powder
1 ½ gm / 2	Black cardamoms *(bari elaichi)*
2	Green cardamoms *(elaichi)*
2	Bayleaves *(tej patta)*
4	Cloves *(laung)*
	Salt to taste
1 tsp	Black cumin seeds *(kala jeera)*

METHOD

◆ Heat the mustard oil till it smokes, and deep fry the cottage cheese and cauliflower till they are light golden brown in colour. Drain and keep aside.

◆ Heat the clarified butter / oil in a separate pan. When hot, reduce the heat and add the aniseed powder, dry ginger powder, turmeric powder, black and green cardamoms, bayleaves and cloves. Stir and add the fried cottage cheese and cauliflower. Add salt and mix well.

◆ Add 1 ½ cups of hot water and cook till the water evaporates. Sprinkle the black cumin seeds and mix well.

Gobi Chaman ▶

MIRCH AUR GOBI KA SALAN

(Cauliflower-capsicum platter)

Serves: 4

INGREDIENTS

500 gm	Cauliflower *(phool gobi)* florets
1	Capsicum *(shimla mirch),* large, deseeded, cubed
150 ml / ¾ cup	Clarified butter *(ghee) /* refined oil
3 gm / 2 tsp	Cumin seeds *(jeera)*
240 gm / 1 cup	Onions *(piyaz),* chopped
54 gm / 3 tbsp	Garlic *(lasan)* paste
54 gm / 3 tbsp	Ginger *(adrak)* paste
18 gm / 6	Green chillies *(hari mirch),* sliced
4 ½ gm / 3 tsp	Red chilli *(lal mirch)* powder
6 gm / 2 tsp	Cumin seed *(jeera)* powder
3 gm / 2 tsp	Coriander seed *(dhaniya)* powder
6 gm / 1 tbsp	Garam masala (standard, see p. 18)
1 gm / 2 tsp	Dry fenugreek *(kasoori methi)*
150 ml / ¾ cup	Yoghurt *(dahi),* whisked
	Salt to taste
1 cup	Tomatoes *(tamatar),* cubed
25 gm / 1 tbsp	Ginger *(adrak)* juliennes

METHOD

◆ Heat the clarified butter / oil in a wok *(kadhai)* and fry the cauliflower florets until they change colour. Remove with a slotted spoon and keep on absorbent paper.

◆ In the same clarified butter / oil, add the cumin seeds, stir and add the onions. Sauté until they are golden brown in colour. Add the garlic and ginger pastes, green chillies, red chilli powder, cumin seed powder, coriander seed powder, garam masala, dry fenugreek, yoghurt and salt. Stir and mix well. Cook until aromatic.

◆ Add the cubed capsicum and tomatoes and cook until the capsicum becomes soft and tender. Then add the cauliflower, stir and simmer for 2-3 minutes. Garnish with ginger juliennes.

VEGETABLES

GOBI JALFREZI

(Cauliflower blended with tomato purée and vinegar)

Serves: 4

INGREDIENTS

600 gm	Cauliflower *(phool gobi)* / broccoli florets
100 ml / ½ cup	Clarified butter *(ghee)* / refined oil
4	Red chillies *(lal mirch)*, dry
2 gm / 1 ½ tsp	Cumin seeds *(jeera)*
	Salt to taste
2 gm / 1 tsp	Peppercorn *(kali mirch)* powder
16 gm / 2 tsp	Ginger *(adrak)* juliennes
100 ml / ½ cup	Tomato *(tamatar)* purée (see p. 24)
15 ml / 1 tbsp	White vinegar *(sirka)*
4 gm / 1 tbsp	Coriander leaves *(hara dhaniya)*, chopped

METHOD

◆ Heat the clarified butter / oil in a wok *(kadhai)*; add the dry red chillies, then stir and add the cumin seeds. When they crackle, add the cauliflower, salt, peppercorn powder and ginger. Stir well. Cover the wok and reduce the heat. Cook on a slow fire until almost tender.

◆ Add the tomato purée and white vinegar. Cook until the cauliflower becomes tender. Garnish with coriander leaves.

106

Gobi Jalfrezi ▶

AVIYAL

(Mixed vegetable)

Serves: 4-6

INGREDIENTS

1 kg	Any choice of mixed vegetables, sliced
100 ml / ½ cup	Clarified butter *(ghee)* / refined oil
3 gm / 1 tsp	Mustard seeds *(sarson)*
16 gm / 2 tsp	Ginger *(adrak)*, minced
2	Garlic *(lasan)* cloves, sliced
120 gm / ½ cup	Onions *(piyaz)*, minced
2	Green chillies *(hari mirch)*, minced
2 gm / 1 ½ tsp	Turmeric *(haldi)* powder
4 ½ gm / 1 tbsp	Coriander seed *(dhaniya)* powder
240 gm / 1 cup	Coconut *(nariyal)*, grated, puréed
	Salt to taste
150 ml / ¾ cup	Coconut milk *(nariyal ka doodh)*
8 gm / 2 tbsp	Coriander leaves *(hara dhaniya)*, chopped

METHOD

◆ Heat the clarified butter / oil in a deep pan and add the mustard seeds. Fry till they splutter. Add the ginger and garlic. Stir and fry for 1 minute. Add the onions and green chillies. Fry till the onions turn golden brown in colour. Add the turmeric and coriander seed powder and mix well.

◆ Put in the sliced vegetables and mix well. Add the coconut purée and salt with the coconut milk. Mix well and bring to a rapid boil. Reduce the heat and cook till the vegetables are tender. Garnish with coriander leaves.

MATTAR KHOYA

(Savoury peas)

Serves: 4-6

INGREDIENTS

125 gm	Wholemilk fudge *(khoya)*, liquidised
700 gm	Peas *(mattar)*, shelled
100 ml / ½ cup	Clarified butter *(ghee)* / refined oil
2 gm / 1 ½ tsp	Cumin seeds *(jeera)*
2	Cloves *(laung)*
1	Cinnamon *(dalchini)* stick, 1"
4 ½ gm / 3 tsp	Red chilli *(lal mirch)* powder
1 ½ gm / 1 tsp	Turmeric *(haldi)* powder
2 gm / 1 ½ tsp	Coriander seed *(dhaniya)* powder
100 ml / ½ cup	Yoghurt *(dahi)*, whisked
	Salt to taste
3 ½ gm / 1 tsp	Brown sugar
2 gm / 1 tsp	Garam masala (see p. 18)

METHOD

◆ Heat the clarified butter / oil; add the cumin seeds, cloves and cinnamon stick. Fry until they crackle. Add the red chilli powder, turmeric and coriander powders, yoghurt, salt and brown sugar. Fry until the clarified butter / oil surfaces.

◆ Add the peas and the wholemilk fudge. Put in 1 cup of hot water and cook until the peas become tender. Sprinkle with the garam masala.

Mattar Khoya ▶

VEGETABLES

PANCHRATTAN KORMA

(Five-in-one vegetable curry)

Serves: 4-6

INGREDIENTS

½ cup	Potatoes *(alu)*, diced
½ cup	Carrots *(gajar)*, diced
½ cup	Peas *(mattar)*, shelled
½ cup	Cauliflower *(phool gobi)* florets
100 ml / ½ cup	Clarified butter *(ghee)* / refined oil
3	Cloves *(laung)*
2	Black cardamoms *(bari elaichi)*, cracked
1	Cinnamon *(dalchini)* stick, 1"
3 gm / 2 tsp	Cumin seeds *(jeera)*
120 gm / ½ cup	Onions *(piyaz)*, finely chopped
15 gm / 2½ tsp	Ginger *(adrak)* paste
6 gm / 3 tsp	Poppy seeds, roasted, made into a paste with a little water
1 cup	Tomatoes *(tamatar)*, chopped
2 ½ gm / 1½ tsp	Turmeric *(haldi)* powder
4 ½ gm / 1½ tsp	Sugar
	Salt to taste
18 gm / 6	Green chillies *(hari mirch)*, sliced
16 gm / 2 tsp	Ginger *(adrak)* juliennes
8 gm / 2 tbsp	Coriander leaves *(hara dhaniya)*

METHOD

◆ Heat the clarified butter / oil in a wok *(kadhai)*; fry the diced potatoes until golden all over. Remove from the clarified butter / oil; prick all over with a fine fork and keep aside.

◆ In the same clarified butter / oil, add the cloves, cardamoms, cinnamon and cumin seeds. When they crackle, add the onions. Sauté until golden brown. Add the ginger and poppy seed pastes. Fry until they change colour. Add the tomatoes, turmeric, sugar and salt. Stir for 1 minute.

◆ Add all the vegetables, potatoes and green chillies; stir until well coated with the gravy. Add 1 cup of water and bring to a boil. Covering the wok, simmer until tender.

◆ Garnish the dish with ginger juliennes and coriander leaves.

DUDHIA KHUMB

(White mushrooms)

Serves: 4-6

INGREDIENTS

500 gm	Mushrooms *(khumb / guchi)*, sliced or whole, without the stem
45 gm / ½ cup	Unsalted butter *(phika makhan)*
180 gm / ¾ cup	Onions *(piyaz)*, chopped
6 gm / 1 tsp	Garlic *(lasan)* paste
3 gm / 1 tsp	Cumin seed *(jeera)* powder
1 ½ gm / 1 tsp	Coriander seed *(dhaniya)* powder
12 gm / 2 tsp	Refined flour *(maida)*
100 ml / ½ cup	Milk
4 gm / 2 tsp	White pepper *(safed mirch)* powder
	Salt to taste

METHOD

◆ Heat the unsalted butter; add the onions and garlic paste. Sauté until translucent. Add the cumin and coriander powders. Stir until well mixed and aromatic. Remove the pan from the heat and cool slightly. Add the refined flour, stirring all the time.

◆ Return the pan to the heat and cook until the colour changes. Add the milk slowly, making sure it is well mixed. Add the mushrooms and cook for 5 to 7 minutes. Put in the white pepper powder and salt. Stir to mix well.

110

Dudhia Khumb ▶

MIRCHI KA SALAN

(Stuffed green chillies)

Serves: 4

INGREDIENTS

1 cup	Green chillies, large, slit and deseeded
400 ml / 2 cups	Clarified butter *(ghee)* / refined oil

Paste 1: Boil in a little water and grind to a fine paste:

120 gm / ½ cup	Coconut *(nariyal)*, grated
¼ cup	Cashewnuts *(kaju)*
18 gm / 4 tbsp	Sesame seeds *(til)*

Paste 2: Mix together to form a paste:

6 gm / 3 tsp	Coriander seeds *(dhaniya)*, roasted and powdered
12 gm / 4 tsp	Cumin seed *(jeera)* powder
3 gm / 2 tsp	Red chilli *(lal mirch)* powder
1 ½ gm / 1 tsp	Turmeric *(haldi)* powder
12 gm / 2 tsp	Ginger *(adrak)* paste
12 gm / 2 tsp	Garlic *(lasan)* paste
½ tsp	Salt

Paste 3: Grind to a paste:

5	Onions *(piyaz)*, sliced, fried until brown

For the baghar:

1 ½ gm / 1 tsp	Cumin seeds *(jeera)*
25	Curry leaves *(meethi neem ke patte)*
3 gm / 1 tsp	Mustard seeds *(sarson)*
1 ½ gm / 1 tsp	Nigella seeds *(kalonji)*
70 gm	Tamarind *(imli)*, soaked in hot water and sieved
	Salt to taste

METHOD

◆ Mix together pastes 1, 2 and 3. Stuff the chillies with the combined pastes. Heat the clarified butter / oil and fry the chillies until they become golden in colour. Remove and keep aside.

◆ Reheat the oil for *baghar* (see p. 20). Add the cumin seeds, curry leaves, mustard seeds and nigella seeds. When they crackle, add the tamarind juice and salt. Heat thoroughly; add the green chillies and simmer for 10 minutes.

BHARWA GUCHI

(Gourmet stuffed mushrooms)

Serves: 4-6

INGREDIENTS

8-10	Morels *(guchi)*, large, dry

For the filling :

¼ cup	Spring onions *(hara piyaz)*, finely chopped and fried until golden
25 gm	Wholemilk fudge *(khoya)*
12 gm / 3 tbsp	Mint *(pudina)* leaves, finely chopped
6 gm / ¼ cup	Coriander leaves *(hara dhaniya)*, finely chopped
30 ml / 2 tbsp	Lemon *(nimbu)* juice
	Salt to taste
100 ml / ½ cup	Clarified butter *(ghee)* / refined oil *(durust* see p. 21)
2	Cloves *(laung)*
2	Green cardamoms *(elaichi)*

For the gravy:

½ cup	Spring onions *(hara piyaz)*, finely minced or grated
12 gm / 2 tsp	Ginger *(adrak)* paste
12 gm / 2 tsp	Garlic *(lasan)* paste
12 gm / 2 tsp	Green chilli *(hari mirch)* paste
60 gm / ¼ cup	Cashewnut *(kaju)* paste, fine
150 ml / ¾ cups	Yoghurt *(dahi)*, thick, whisked
	Salt to taste
3 gm / 1½ tsp	Garam masala (fragrant, see p. 18)
¼ gm / ¼ tsp	Saffron *(kesar)*, soaked in 3 tbsp warm milk

112

METHOD

◆ Wash and hydrate the morels in warm water and then boil in fresh water for 10 minutes.
◆ Drain the morels; mix together the filling mixture and stuff the morels with it.
◆ Heat the clarified butter / oil *(durust)* to a smoking point. Remove from heat and cool slightly. Add the cloves and green cardamoms and fry till they change colour. Remove from the clarified butter / oil and discard.
◆ **For the gravy,** heat the clarified butter / oil *(durust)* in a large pan. Add the onions and sauté until they become translucent. Add the ginger and garlic pastes and stir until the water evaporates and they change their colour. Add the cashewnut paste and fry until well blended and the colour changes. Reduce the heat and add the yoghurt and salt. Stir and simmer until a sauce-like consistency is achieved. Add the fragrant garam masala and the saffron milk. Stir to mix well.
◆ Add the stuffed morels and ¼ cup of hot water. Simmer for 10 minutes, coating the morels with the gravy.

Bharwa Guchi ▶

KHATHI~MEETHI GOBI

(Honey-tamarind cabbage)

Serves: 4-6

INGREDIENTS

½	Cabbage *(band gobi)*, large, cut into small strips
100 ml / ½ cup	Clarified butter *(ghee)* / refined oil
1 ½ gm / 1 tsp	Coriander seed *(dhaniya)* powder
4 gm / 2 tsp	Garam masala (standard, see p. 18)
2 gm / 1 tsp	Peppercorn *(kali mirch)* powder
50 gm	Tamarind *(imli)*, soaked in water to extract ¾ cup
5 ml / 1 tbsp	Vinegar *(sirka)*
	Salt to taste
10 ml / 2 tbsp	Honey *(shahad)*, clear

METHOD

◆ Heat the clarified butter / oil and remove from heat. Add the coriander powder, garam masala and peppercorn powder. Stir. Return the pan to the heat and add the cabbage, tamarind extract and vinegar. Bring to a boil, then add salt and honey. Cook until the cabbage is done.

KHAJOOR-KISHMISH KA SALAN

(Sumptuous cashewnut, raisin and almond curry)

Serves: 4

INGREDIENTS

60 gm / ½ cup	Sultanas (kishmish), soaked in water for 2 hours, drained
15 gm / 12	Cashewnuts (kaju), halved
½ cup	Dates (khajoor), seedless and halved
10 gm / 12	Almonds (badam), blanched, peeled and halved

For the paste:

150 gm / ½ cup	Onion (piyaz) paste
30 gm / 1½ tbsp	Tomato (tamatar) purée
6 gm / 1 tsp	Garlic (lasan) paste
6 gm / 1 tsp	Ginger (adrak) paste
3 gm / 1 tsp	Cumin seed (jeera) powder
100 ml / ½ cup	Clarified butter (ghee) / refined oil
2 gm / 1½ tsp	Turmeric (haldi) powder
1 ½ gm / 1 tsp	Red chilli (lal mirch) powder
2 gm / 1 tsp	Garam masala (see p. 18)
7 gm / 2 tsp	Treacle or brown sugar
2 gm / 1 tsp	Dry mango powder (amchur)
	Salt to taste

METHOD

◆ Mix the ingredients for the paste together. Heat the clarified butter / oil and add the paste. Fry until brown in colour. Add the turmeric, red chilli powder, garam masala, treacle, dry mango powder and salt. Stir for 30 seconds.

◆ Add the sultanas, cashewnuts, dates, and almonds. Add ¾ cup of warm water and cook until the nuts become soft and tender. When ready to serve, the dish should have a thick gravy.

Khajoor-Kishmish Ka Salan ▶

LASAN KARI

(Garlic curry)

Serves: 4-6

INGREDIENTS

250 gm	Garlic (lasan), whole, large cloves
10	Onions (piyaz), small, whole
24 gm / 8	Green chillies (hari mirch), slit in two
100 ml / ½ cup	Clarified butter (ghee) / refined oil
3 gm / 1 tsp	Fenugreek seeds (methi dana)
6	Curry leaves (meethi neem ke patte)
1 ½ gm / 1 tsp	Red chilli (lal mirch) powder
1 gm / ½ tsp	Turmeric (haldi) powder
300 ml / 1½ cup	Coconut milk (nariyal ka doodh), thick
	Salt to taste
15 ml / 3 tsp	Lemon (nimbu) juice

METHOD

◆ Heat the clarified butter / oil; add the garlic cloves, whole onions and green chillies. Fry until light golden in colour. Remove with a slotted spoon and keep aside.

◆ In the same clarified butter / oil, add the fenugreek seeds and curry leaves. Fry until the seeds crackle. Reduce the heat and add the red chilli and turmeric powders. Stir and add the coconut milk and salt. Bring to a boil and add the garlic, onions and green chillies. Cook until the garlic cloves become tender.

◆ Add the lemon juice just before serving.

DAL MAHARANI

(Pulses with a pizazz)

Serves: 4-6

INGREDIENTS

300 gm / 2½ cups	Split black gram (urad dal)
75 gm / ½ cup	Red kidney beans (rajmah)
18 gm / 3 tsp	Garlic (lasan) paste
25 gm / 4 tsp	Ginger (adrak) paste
3 gm / 2 tsp	Red chilli (lal mirch) powder
200 ml / 1 cup	Tomato (tamatar) purée
45 gm / ½ cup	Unsalted butter (phika makhan)
150 ml / ¾ cup	Cream
	Salt to taste

METHOD

◆ Clean, wash and soak the split black gram and the beans in plenty of water overnight or for at least 12 hours.
◆ Wash the gram and beans under cold running water. Heat 1 ½ litres of water in an open pressure cooker. When it starts boiling, add the gram and beans. Close the cooker and cook for 12 minutes. Remove from heat and cool.
◆ Open the pressure cooker carefully and with a wooden spoon, mash the split black gram and beans on the sides of the pan by stirring the spoon rapidly. When they are partly broken, add the garlic and ginger pastes, red chilli powder and the tomato puree. Add 1 ½ cups of warm water, mix well and once again, put the cooker uncovered, back on heat. Bring to a boil and simmer for 30 minutes, stirring occasionally, making sure that the gram and beans do not stick to the bottom of the cooker.
◆ Add the butter, stirring until it is completely absorbed. Add the cream and stir. Cook for another 10 minutes or until the mixture is of a thick consistency.
(Note. Normally this dish takes close to 12 to 14 hours to cook. The short cut given here has been arrived at after thorough experimentation, and the result does justice to this age-old recipe.)

Dal Maharani ▶

AMRITSARI DAL

(Pleasing pulses)

Serves: 4-6

INGREDIENTS

200 gm / 1 cup	Split black gram (urad dal)
80 gm / ½ cup	Split Bengal gram (chana dal)
	Salt to taste
50 gm / 2 tbsp	Ginger (adrak), chopped
25 gm / 2 tbsp	Garlic (lasan), chopped
45 gm / ½ cup	Unsalted butter
100 ml / ½ cup	Clarified butter (ghee) / refined oil
120 gm / ½ cup	Onions (piyaz), chopped
18 gm / 6	Green chillies (hari mirch), chopped
¼ cup	Tomatoes (tamatar), chopped
4 gm / 1 tbsp	Mint (pudina) leaves

METHOD

◆ Wash and soak the split pulses in plenty of water for 1 hour. Drain.
◆ Heat 1 litre of water in a large pan; add salt and the lentils. Bring to a boil, reduce heat and keep removing the scum that surfaces. Add 1 ½ tbsp of ginger, 1 ½ tbsp of garlic and unsalted butter. Cover and cook until the pulses are cooked and a little water remains. Mash the pulses against the sides of the pan with a large spoon.
◆ Heat the clarified butter / oil in a frying pan; add onions and fry until light brown. Add the remaining ginger and garlic and fry until they too turn brown. Add the green chillies, tomatoes and mint leaves. Cook until the tomatoes are well blended and mashed. Transfer to the cooked pulses. Stir.

RAJMAH ANARDANA

(Kidney beans flavoured with pomegranate seeds)

Serves: 4-6

INGREDIENTS

350 gm / 2 cups	Red kidney beans *(rajmah)*, soaked in plenty of water for 12-15 hours, drained, washed and kept aside
45 gm / ½ cup	Unsalted butter *(phika makhan)*
3	Onions *(piyaz)*, medium size, raw, paste
12 gm / 2 tsp	Ginger *(adrak)* paste
12 gm / 2 tsp	Garlic *(lasan)* paste
100 ml / ½ cup	Tomato *(tamatar)* purée
3 gm / 2 tsp	Coriander seed *(dhaniya)* powder
3 gm / 2 tsp	Red chilli *(lal mirch)* powder
1 ½ gm / 1 tsp	Turmeric *(haldi)* powder
3 gm / 1 tsp	Cumin seed *(jeera)* powder

For the paste:

4	Cloves *(laung)*
2	Cinnamon *(dalchini)* sticks, 1"
	Salt to taste
25 gm / 2 tbsp	Pomegranate seeds *(anardana)*, ground

METHOD

◆ Heat 6 cups of water, add the red kidney beans and cook until tender. Stir rapidly mashing the beans against the sides of the pan.

◆ Heat the unsalted butter; add the onion, garlic and ginger pastes. Fry until brown. Add the tomato purée, stir for 30 seconds, then add the coriander seed powder, red chilli powder, turmeric powder, cumin seed powder, clove and cinnamon paste and salt. Cook for two minutes.

◆ Add the masala to the cooked kidney beans and bring to a boil. Stir and simmer for 5 minutes.

◆ Add the ground pomegranate seeds just before serving.

Rajmah Anardana ▶

DHABA DAL

(Rich and buttery split black gram)

Serves: 4-6

INGREDIENTS

300 gm / 1½ cups	Split black gram *(urad dal)*
1 ½ gm / 1 tsp	Turmeric *(haldi)* powder
3 gm / 2 tsp	Red chilli *(lal mirch)* powder
	Salt to taste

For the baghar:

65 gm / ¾ cup	Unsalted butter
3 gm / 2 tsp	Cumin seeds *(jeera)*
240 gm / 1 cup	Onions *(piyaz)*, chopped
18 gm / 6	Green chillies *(hari mirch)*, halved
25 gm / 1 tbsp	Ginger *(adrak)*, chopped
4 ½ gm / 2 tsp	Garam masala (see p. 18)
½ cup	Tomatoes *(tamatar)*, chopped
50 ml / ¼ cup	Lemon *(nimbu)* juice
22 gm / ¼ cup	Butter
6 gm / 1 tsp	Ginger *(adrak)* paste
6 gm / 1 tsp	Garlic *(lasan)* paste

METHOD

◆ Wash and clean the split black gram and boil in water, adding the turmeric, red chilli powder and salt. Cook until tender. Drain any excess water. Keep aside.

◆ Heat the unsalted butter; add the cumin seeds and fry until they crackle. Add the onions, green chillies and chopped ginger. Fry until brown in colour. Add the boiled black gram.

◆ Put in the garam masala, tomatoes and lemon juice. Stirring, cook for one minute. Add the ginger and garlic pastes. Mix, adding ½ a cup of water. Bring to a boil and then add a quarter cup of butter, stirring until completely absorbed.

TELIA MA

(Split black gram—gourmet accompaniment for a delectable meal)

Serves: 4-6

INGREDIENTS

200 gm / 1 cup	Split black gram *(urad dal),* soaked in water for 12 hours
1 ½ gm / 1 tsp	Turmeric *(haldi)* powder
	Salt to taste
200 ml / 1 cup	Yoghurt *(dahi),* whisked
200 ml / 1 cup	Clarified butter *(ghee)* / refined oil
2 gm / 4	Black cardamoms *(bari elaichi)*
2	Cinnamon *(dalchini)* sticks, 1"
3 gm / 1½ tsp	Cumin *(jeera)* seeds
6	Onions *(piyaz),* sliced
6	Garlic *(lasan)* cloves, chopped
16 gm / 2 tsp	Ginger *(adrak),* chopped
1 cup	Tomatoes *(tamatar),* chopped
2 gm / 1½ tsp	Coriander seed *(dhaniya)* powder
2 gm / 1½ tsp	Red chilli *(lal mirch)* powder

METHOD

◆ Drain and wash the split black gram. Heat 3 ½ cups of water and bring to a boil. Add the black gram, turmeric and salt. Cook until it becomes tender and a little water remains. Remove from heat and cool.

◆ Pour the cooled black gram into a large plate and add the yoghurt. Keep aside.

◆ Heat the clarified butter / oil; add the black cardamoms, cinnamon sticks and cumin seeds. When they crackle, add the chopped onions, garlic and ginger. Fry until golden brown. Add the chopped tomatoes, coriander powder and red chilli powder. Cook until the tomatoes are well blended and the clarified butter / oil comes to the surface.

◆ Add the black gram and yoghurt and cook on a slow fire until all the liquid is absorbed.

Telia Ma ▶

HALEEM SHAKAHARI

(A balanced vegetarian one-dish meal)

Serves 4-6

INGREDIENTS

270 gm / 1½ cups	Broken wheat or wheat porridge *(dalia)*
80 gm / 4 tbsp	Split red gram *(toovar, toor* or *arhar dal)*
40 gm / 2 tbsp	Lentils *(masoor dal)*
45 gm / 2 tbsp	Split Bengal gram *(chana dal)*
100 ml / ½ cup	Clarified butter *(ghee)* / refined oil
180 gm / 1½ cups	Onions *(piyaz),* sliced
36 gm / 2 tbsp	Garlic *(lasan)* paste
36 gm / 2 tbsp	Ginger *(adrak)* paste
3 gm / 2 tsp	Coriander seed *(dhaniya)* powder
6 gm / 2 tsp	Cumin seed *(jeera)* powder
3 gm / 2 tsp	Red chilli *(lal mirch)* powder
1 ½ gm / 1 tsp	Turmeric *(haldi)* powder
	Salt to taste
1200 ml / 6 cups	Water
150 gm	Cauliflower *(phool gobi),* small florets
50 gm	Peas *(mattar),* shelled
50 gm	Carrots *(gajar),* cut into 1" pieces
2	Capsicums *(shimla mirch),* sliced, with the seeds removed
4 gm / 2 tsp	Garam masala (standard. p. 18)

METHOD

◆ Separately soak in water the broken wheat, split red gram lentils and split Bengal gram overnight or for at least 12 hours.

◆ Wash the above well and remove the husk from the wheat. Drain and keep aside for 30 minutes.

◆ Heat the clarified butter / oil in a large pan. When hot, add the onions and sauté until they are golden brown. Add the garlic and ginger pastes. Fry until brown. Add the coriander seed powder, cumin seed powder, red chilli powder, turmeric, salt, broken wheat and the other lentils. Mix well.

◆ Add water, cover and cook over very low heat for 1 ½ hours. When cooked, the wheat should be pulpy and the lentils tender. Add the cauliflower, peas, carrots and capsicums. Stir and add the garam masala. Cook until the vegetables are tender and the clarified butter / oil comes to the surface.

METHI MASOOR KI DAL

(Lentils flavoured with fenugreek)

Serves: 4-6

INGREDIENTS

500 gm	Fenugreek *(methi)* leaves, washed and chopped finely
100 gm / ½ cup	Lentils *(masoor dal)*
100 ml / ½ cup	Clarified butter *(ghee)* / refined oil
90 gm / ¾ cup	Onions *(piyaz),* sliced
8 gm / 1 tsp	Ginger *(adrak),* minced
4 gm / 1 tsp	Garlic *(lasan),* minced
4 ½ gm / 3 tsp	Red chilli *(lal mirch)* powder
1 gm / ½ tsp	Turmeric *(haldi)* powder
	Salt to taste

METHOD

◆ Heat the clarified butter / oil in a pan. When hot, add the onions and sauté until they turn golden brown. Add the ginger and garlic. Cook until brown. Add the red chilli powder and turmeric.

◆ Put in the fenugreek leaves and the lentils and cook until the leaves change colour. Add salt to taste and 1 cup of water. Cook over low heat until the water dries and the lentils become tender.

Methi Masoor Ki Dal ▲

PUNJABI CHANA

(Spicy chick peas)

Serves: 4-6

INGREDIENTS

300 gm / 1½ cups	Chick peas *(kabuli chana)*, soaked in water for 2 hours
3 gm / ½ tsp	Bicarbonate of soda
	Salt to taste
100 ml / ½ cup	Clarified butter *(ghee)* / refined oil
36 gm / 6 tsp	Garlic *(lasan)* paste
10	Red chillies *(lal mirch)*, whole, ground with a little water
12 gm / 6 tsp	Coriander seeds *(dhaniya)*, ground with a little water
4 cups	Tomatoes *(tamatar)*, chopped
18 gm / 6	Green chillies *(hari mirch)*, slit
20 gm / ¼ cup	Ginger *(adrak)*, chopped finely
45 ml / 3 tbsp	Lemon *(nimbu)* juice
5 gm / 2½ tsp	Garam masala (see p. 18)
½ gm / 1 tsp	Dry fenugreek leaves *(kasoori methi)*

METHOD

◆ Drain and wash the chick peas. Boil in sufficient water with the bicarbonate of soda and salt until the chick peas become tender. Drain the water and keep aside.

◆ Heat the clarified butter / oil in a pan; add the garlic paste and fry until golden in colour. Add the red chilli and coriander seed pastes. Stir fry until the water evaporates. Add the chopped tomatoes, green chillies and three quarters of the chopped ginger. Bring to a boil; reduce heat and cook until the clarified butter / oil comes to the surface.

◆ Add the cooked chick peas and mix. Cook for 5 minutes, mixing well. Add the lemon juice, garam masala and the dry fenugreek leaves. Mix well. Sprinkle the remaining chopped ginger on the top.

Punjabi Chana ▶

DAL KABULI

(Lemon-flavoured pulses)

Serves: 4-6

INGREDIENTS

250 gm / 1¼ cups	Split black gram *(urad dal)*, soaked in water for 3 hours
100 ml / ½ cup	Clarified butter *(ghee)* / refined oil
36 gm / 6 tsp	Garlic *(lasan)* paste
2 gm / 1½ tsp	Red chilli *(lal mirch)* powder
8 gm / 5 tsp	Coriander seed *(dhaniya)* powder
3 ½ cups	Tomatoes *(tamatar)*, chopped
12 gm / ½ cup	Coriander leaves *(hara dhaniya)*, chopped
6	Green chillies *(hari mirch)*, chopped
64 gm / 8 tsp	Ginger *(adrak)*, chopped
80 gm / 8 tbsp	Unsalted butter
4 ½ gm / 2 tsp	Garam masala (see p. 18)
30 ml / 2 tbsp	Lemon *(nimbu)* juice
	Salt to taste

METHOD

◆ Wash the split black gram. Boil in 3 litres of water and cook until tender. Drain the excess water.

◆ Heat the clarified butter / oil; add the garlic paste and fry until golden brown. Add the red chilli and coriander seed powder. Stir for a few seconds, then add the tomatoes. Bring to a boil and add the coriander leaves, green chillies and ginger. Cook on medium heat until the oil surfaces.

◆ Add the black gram and stir for 5 minutes. Put in the salt, add the butter and stir until fully absorbed. Add the garam masala and lemon juice. Add ½ cup of water and cook on medium heat for another 5 minutes, mashing the black gram against the sides of the pan.

KHAREE MASOOR KE DAL

(Lentils flavoured with curry leaves)

Serves: 4

INGREDIENTS

100 gm / ½ cup	Lentils *(masoor dal),* picked and washed
100 ml / ½ cup	Clarified butter *(ghee)* / refined oil
240 gm / 1 cup	Onions *(piyaz),* finely chopped
12 gm / 4	Green chillies *(hari mirch),* chopped
6 gm / 1 tsp	Garlic *(lasan)* paste
6 gm / 1 tsp	Ginger *(adrak)* paste
1 ½ gm / 1 tsp	Red chilli *(lal mirch)* powder
1 ½ gm / 1 tsp	Turmeric *(haldi)* powder
12	Curry leaves *(meethi neem ke patte)*
	Salt to taste
1	Lemon *(nimbu),* juice

METHOD

◆ Heat the clarified butter / oil; add the onions, green chillies, garlic and ginger pastes, red chilli powder, turmeric powder and the curry leaves. Fry for 3 minutes.

◆ Add the washed lentils and salt. Fry for 4 minutes. Put in 1 cup of hot water. Bring to a boil, cover and simmer until the lentils are tender and the clarified butter / oil surfaces. Add the lemon juice and stir.

Kharee Masoor Ke Dal ▶

DAL LUCKNAVI

(Tangy red gram)

Serves: 4-6

INGREDIENTS

165 gm / 1 cup	Split red gram *(toovar, toor* or *arhar dal)*
1 lt	Water
	Salt to taste
1 ½ gm / 1 tsp	Red chilli *(lal mirch)* powder
1 ½ gm / 1 tsp	Turmeric *(haldi)* powder
18 gm / 1 tbsp	Garlic *(lasan)* paste
45 gm / ½ cup	Butter *(makhan)*
100 ml / ½ cup	Cream
200 ml / 1 cup	Yoghurt *(dahi),* whisked
2 gm / 1 tsp	Cumin seeds *(jeera)*
120 gm / ½ cup	Onions *(piyaz),* finely chopped
12 gm / 1 tbsp	Garlic *(lasan),* chopped
15 ml / 3 tsp	Lemon *(nimbu)* juice
2 gm / 1 ½ tsp	Peppercorn *(kali mirch)* powder

METHOD

◆ Wash the split red gram and boil in 1 litre water with the salt, red chilli powder and turmeric. Cook until the lentils are tender and the grain is broken and of a semi-thick consistency.

◆ Reduce the heat and add the garlic paste; uncover the pan and cook for a further 10 minutes, stirring all the time.

◆ Add half the butter, cream and yoghurt. Stir until all these ingredients are completely absorbed. Cover the pan and cook for a further 10 minutes.

◆ While the lentils are cooking, heat the remaining butter in another pan. When heated, add the cumin seeds and sauté until they crackle. Add the chopped onions and chopped garlic and fry until they become translucent; then add to the lentils and stir.

◆ Cook the lentils for another 5 minutes. Add the lemon juice and peppercorn powder and stir.

TIL AUR CURRY PATTA BHATH

(Basmati rice seasoned with sesame seeds)

Serves: 4-6

INGREDIENTS

400 gm / 2 cups	Basmati rice, cleaned, soaked in water for 1 hour, drained
700 ml / 3½ cups	Water
9 gm / 2 tsp	Salt
45 ml / 3 tbsp	Sesame *(til)* oil
18	Curry leaves *(meethi neem ke patte)*
3 gm / 1 tsp	Mustard seeds *(sarson)*
2 gm / 1 tsp	Cumin seeds *(jeera)*
¾ cup	Sesame seeds *(til)*
30 ml / 2 tbsp	Lemon *(nimbu)* juice

METHOD

◆ Put the drained rice, water and salt in a heavy pan. Bring to a boil. Reduce heat and cover the pan with a lid and cook until the rice is cooked and the water is absorbed. Keep warm and put aside.

◆ Heat the sesame oil in a saucepan. When hot, add the curry leaves, mustard seeds and the cumin seeds. Fry until the leaves change colour and the mustard and cumin seeds crackle. Reduce the heat and add the sesame seeds and fry until they are evenly golden brown.

◆ Add this seasoning with the lemon juice to the cooked rice. Mix well, taking care that the rice grains do not break.

126

Til Aur Curry Patta Bhath ▶

PUDINA AUR DHANIYA CHAWAL

(Mint and coriander-flavoured rice)

Serves: 4-6

INGREDIENTS

400 gm / 2 cups	Basmati rice, washed and soaked in water for 30 minutes, drained
½ gm / ½ tsp	Saffron *(kesar)* strands
100 ml / ½ cup	Clarified butter *(ghee)* / refined oil
1	Cinnamon *(dalchini)* stick, 2"
4	Cloves *(laung)*
18 gm / 2 tsp	Ginger *(adrak)*, minced
300 ml / 1½ cups	Yoghurt *(dahi)*, whisked
1	Onion *(piyaz)*, large, finely chopped
12 gm / 3 tbsp	Coriander leaves *(hara dhaniya)*, finely chopped
4 gm / 1 tbsp	Mint leaves *(hara pudina)*, finely chopped
4 gm / 2 tsp	White pepper powder
	Salt to taste

METHOD

◆ Put the drained rice in a pan and add water to just about cover it. Add saffron and boil for 10 minutes. Remove from heat and drain all the excess water. Keep aside.

◆ Heat the clarified butter / oil; add the cinnamon and cloves. Sauté until they crackle. Add the ginger and stir. Add the drained rice and stir until it is well coated with the oil. Add the whisked yoghurt, chopped onions, coriander and mint leaves, white pepper powder and salt. Put on very low heat and cover. Cook until the rice is cooked and the yoghurt absorbed.

SHAHJEHANI BIRYANI

(Biryani à la cuisine royale)

Serves: 12-14

RICE

128

INGREDIENTS

For the meat:

2 kg	Lamb / mutton, deboned, cubed
100 ml / ½ cup	Clarified butter *(ghee)*
225 gm / ¾ cup	Onions *(piyaz)*, made into a paste
36 gm / 2 tbsp	Ginger *(adrak)* paste
36 gm / 2 tbsp	Garlic *(lasan)* paste
25 gm / 1½ tbsp	Poppy seed *(khus khus)* paste
12 gm / 12	Red chillies *(lal mirch)*, dry, ground to a paste with water
60 gm / 4 tbsp	Almonds *(badam)*, blanched, peeled, ground to a paste
9 gm / 3 tsp	Cumin seed *(jeera)* powder
3 gm / 1½ tsp	Green cardamom seed *(elaichi)* powder
2 gm / 1½ tsp	Cinnamon *(dalchini)* powder
1 gm / ½ tsp	Nutmeg *(jaiphal)* powder
1 ½ tsp	Clove *(laung)* powder
3 gm / 2 tsp	Peppercorn *(kali mirch)* powder
100 ml / ½ cup	Yoghurt *(dahi)*
	Salt to taste

For the rice:

1 kg / 5 cups	Basmati rice, washed and soaked in water for 30 minutes, and drained
1600 ml / 8 cups	Water
2	Cinnamon *(dalchini)* sticks, 1"
8	Green cardamom pods *(elaichi)*, cracked
5 ml / 1 tsp	Vetivier *(kewra)* essence
½ gm / ½ tsp	Saffron *(kesar)* strands, soaked in ½ cup of hot milk
150 ml / ¾ cup	Cream
2 gm / 1½ tsp	Cumin seeds *(jeera)*

For the garnishing:

2	Onions *(piyaz)*, large, sliced and fried until golden brown
60 gm / ½ cup	Sultanas *(kishmish)*, fried

METHOD

To cook the meat:

◆ Heat the clarified butter; add the blended mixture of the pastes and spices for the meat, stirring constantly until an aroma rises and the clarified butter separates. Add ½ a cup of water and simmer until it evaporates.

◆ Add the meat with the salt. Stir and coat with the paste evenly. *Bhunao* (see p. 21) until brown in colour. Add a little water if the meat sticks to the bottom of the pan. Add the yoghurt and water. Cook until the meat becomes tender and there is a very thick gravy.

To cook the rice:

◆ Put rice in a pan and add the water, cinnamon, cardamom and *kewra*. Bring to a boil and reduce heat, cooking until the rice is almost tender and the water is absorbed.

◆ In a heavy, greased, oven-proof casserole, spread half the rice. Pour half the saffron liquid, half the cream and half the black cumin seeds over it. Then spread the cooked meat evenly. Repeat this process a second time.

◆ Cover the dish tightly, pressing down with aluminium foil. Put a lid and bake for 35 minutes in an oven which has been preheated at 160⁰C / 325⁰F. Garnish with the fried onions and sultanas.

KEEMA KI BIRYANI

(Royal mince Biryani)

Serves: 4

INGREDIENTS

400 gm / 2 cups	Basmati rice, washed and soaked in water for 1 hour, drained
	Salt to taste
500 gm	Lamb / mutton, minced
100 ml / ½ cup	Clarified butter *(ghee)* / refined oil
60 gm / ½ cup	Onions *(piyaz)*, thinly sliced
4 ½ gm / 3 tsp	Red chilli *(lal mirch)* powder
9 gm / 2 tbsp	Coriander seed *(dhaniya)* powder
12 gm / 2 tsp	Garlic *(lasan)* paste
12 gm / 2 tsp	Ginger *(adrak)* paste
100 ml / ½ cup	Yoghurt *(dahi)*
	Salt to taste
4 ½ gm / 2 tsp	Garam masala (standard, see p. 18)

Mix together:

16 gm / 20	Almonds *(badam)*, blanched, peeled and sliced
32 gm / 60	Sultanas *(kishmish)*, cut into half
45 gm / 3 tbsp	Wholemilk fudge *(khoya)*
60 ml / 4 tbsp	Lemon *(nimbu)* juice
450 ml / 2¼ cups	Milk

METHOD

◆ Boil the rice with the salt in plenty of water. When cooked, drain the excess water and keep the rice aside to cool.

◆ Heat the clarified butter / oil; add the onions and fry until golden brown. Add the mince with the red chilli powder, coriander seed powder, garlic and ginger pastes, yoghurt and salt. Cook until the meat is well browned, adding 2 tablespoons of water, as and when required to avoid it sticking to the bottom of the pan *(bhunao)*. Add water and cook until tender and no liquid remains. Add the garam masala.

◆ In a greased, heavy-bottomed pan (not too large), spread a layer of rice evenly and sprinkle half the milk over it. Spread half the cooked mince evenly over the rice. Cover the mince with another layer of rice. Spread the almonds-sultanas, wholemilk fudge, lemon juice mixture over this, and then spread the balance of the mince. Cover with rice once again. Sprinkle with the rest of the milk.

◆ Cover the dish with aluminium foil and a lid thereafter. Put the pan on very low heat and cook on *dum* (see p. 21) for half an hour.

Keema Ki Biryani ▶

MATTARWALE CHAWAL

(Pea pilaf)

Serves: 4

INGREDIENTS

500 gm / 1½ cups	Basmati rice, washed and soaked in water for 1 hour, drained
30 ml / 2 tbsp	Clarified butter *(ghee)*
1 ½ gm / 1 tsp	Cumin seeds *(jeera)*
120 gm / 1 cup	Onions *(piyaz)*, finely sliced
2 gm / 1 tsp	Garam masala (fragrant, see p. 18)
200 gm / 1½ cups	Peas *(mattar)*, shelled
	Salt to taste
120 gm / 1 cup	Onions *(piyaz)*, sliced, fried golden brown

METHOD

◆ Heat the clarified butter; add the cumin seeds. When they crackle, add the chopped onions and fry until golden. Add the garam masala, stir and add the rice. Fry for two minutes, until the rice is well coated with clarified butter.

◆ Add water and bring to a boil. Reduce the heat and add the shelled peas and salt and stir. Cover and cook until all the water is absorbed and the rice and peas are done. Garnish with the fried onions.

MURGH PULAO

(Chicken rice)

Serves: 4-6

INGREDIENTS

8 pieces	Chicken, without skin
400 gm / 2 cups	Basmati rice, washed, soaked in water for 30 minutes and drained
100 ml / ½ cup	Clarified butter *(ghee)* / refined oil
180 gm / ¾ cup	Onions *(piyaz)*, finely chopped
1"	Ginger *(adrak)*, finely chopped
3	Garlic *(lasan)* cloves, crushed
12 gm / 4	Green chillies *(hari mirch)*, finely chopped

Combine together and keep aside:

1 ½ gm / 1 tsp	Turmeric *(haldi)* powder
1 gm / ¾ tsp	Red chilli *(lal mirch)* powder
4 ½ gm / 1 tbsp	Coriander seed *(dhaniya)* powder
1 ½ gm / ¾ tsp	Peppercorn *(kali mirch)* powder
150 ml / ¾ cup	Yogurt *(dahi)*
1	Lemon *(nimbu)*, juice
	Salt to taste

METHOD

◆ Heat the clarified butter / oil in a heavy-bottomed pan over moderate heat and when the clarified butter / oil becomes hot, add the onions and sauté until translucent. Then add the ginger, garlic, cloves and green chillies and continue frying until all of them turn golden brown.

◆ Add the chicken pieces and increase the heat. Fry, turning them frequently, until they are golden all over. Add the mixed ingredients and stir, mixing them well. Cover the pan, lower the heat and cook until the chicken is tender.

◆ Uncover the pan, increase the heat to high and stir in the rice. Mix the rice and add 3 ½ cups of very hot water. Cover the pan and bring to a boil. Reduce the heat to low and simmer until the rice is cooked and all the liquid has been absorbed.

NARIYAL BHATH

(Coconut-milk rice)

Serves: 4

INGREDIENTS

400 gm / 2 cups	Basmati rice, washed and soaked in water for 30 minutes and drained
45 ml / 3 tbsp	Clarified butter *(ghee)* / refined oil
120 gm / 1 cup	Onions *(piyaz)*, sliced
10	Curry leaves *(meethi neem ke patte)*
10	Peppercorns *(kali mirch)*
6	Green cardamoms *(elaichi)*
6	Cloves *(laung)*
800 ml / 4 cups	Coconut milk *(nariyal ka doodh)*, thick
	Salt to taste

METHOD

◆ Heat the clarified butter / oil; add the onions, curry leaves, peppercorns, cardamoms and cloves. Fry together until the onions turn golden brown.

◆ Add the rice and stir until it is evenly coated with clarified butter / oil. Add the coconut milk and salt. Cook until the rice is tender.

AKHA JEERA CHAAMP PULAO

(Pilaf with masala ribs)

Serves: 6-8

INGREDIENTS

1 kg	Lamb / mutton ribs, double
5 each	Green cardamoms *(elaichi)*, Cloves *(laung)*
4	Cinnamon *(dalchini)* sticks, 2" each
1 tsp	Peppercorns *(kali mirch)*, Salt to taste
200 ml / 1 cup	Butter *(makhan)* / refined oil
3 gm / 2 tsp	Cumin seeds *(jeera)*
3	Onions *(piyaz)*, medium, sliced
3 gm / 1 ½ tsp	Garam masala (see p. 18)

Make a fine paste with a little water:

24 gm / 4 tsp	Garlic *(lasan)* and ginger *(adrak)* paste
36 gm / 12-13	Green chillies *(hari mirch)*
8 gm / 2 tbsp	Coriander leaves *(hara dhaniya)*, fresh
4 gm / 1 tbsp	Mint *(pudina)* leaves, fresh
600 gm / 3 cups	Basmati rice, washed and soaked in water for 30 minutes and then drained

METHOD

◆ Cook the ribs in 5 cups of water with the cardamoms, cloves, cinnamon, peppercorns and salt till it is tender. Sieve the stock into another pan. Keep the ribs aside for use later.

◆ Heat the butter / oil in a pan on low heat until the foam subsides. Add the cumin seeds and fry for a few seconds. Increase the heat and cook the sliced onions till golden. Add the garam masala and fine paste; cook until the water evaporates.

◆ Add the cooked ribs and stir. *Bhunao* (see p. 21) twice, adding a few tbsp of water. Add the stock, topping up with warm water to make 5 ½ cups. Bring to a rapid boil and add the rice. Stir to mix well. Cover the pan and lower the heat. Cook until the rice is cooked and the stock absorbed.

▲ *Akha Jeera Chaamp Pulao*

GAJRELA

(Carrot milk pudding)

Serves: 4-6

INGREDIENTS

1 kg	Carrots *(gajar)*, scraped and grated finely
2 ½ lt	Milk
285 gm / 1 ½ cups	Sugar
200 ml / 1 cup	Clarified butter *(ghee)* / refined oil
60 gm / ½ cup	Sultanas *(kishmish)*
65 gm / ½ cup	Almonds *(badam)*, blanched, peeled and sliced
50 gm approx/½ cup	Charoli seeds *(chironji)*

METHOD

◆ Boil the grated carrots in the milk, stirring regularly until the milk is completely absorbed. Reduce the heat and add the sugar and clarified butter / oil. Fry until the sugar is dissolved and the carrots turn deep red in colour. Add the sultanas, almonds and charoli seeds.

Gajrela ▶

PHIRNI

(Ground rice dessert flavoured with cardamoms and pistachios)

Serves: 4-6

INGREDIENTS

600 ml / 3 cups	Milk
3 tbsp	Rice *(chawal)*, ground
75 gm / 6 tbsp	Sugar
1 gm / ½ tsp	Green cardamom seeds *(elaichi)*, ground
15 ml / 1 tbsp	Vetivier *(kewra)* essence
30 gm / 2 tbsp	Pistachios *(pista)*, blanched and sliced

METHOD

◆ Mix 4 tablespoons of milk with the ground rice. Form a smooth paste. Keep aside. Bring the rest of the milk to a boil and add the sugar, stirring until the sugar is dissolved.
◆ Remove the pan from the heat and add the ground rice paste. Stir well and return to the heat. Stir constantly until the mixture thickens. Boil for 5 minutes, stirring. Remove the pan from the heat. Add the ground cardamoms and vetivier essence; mix well.
◆ Pour the mixture into individual dessert bowls and garnish with pistachios. Chill and serve.

KHEER

(Sweetened rice pudding)

Serves: 4-6

INGREDIENTS

1 cup	Basmati rice, soaked in plenty of water for 30 minutes, washed and drained
2 lt	Milk
5	Green cardamoms *(elaichi)*, cracked
½ cup	Sultanas *(kishmish)*, soaked in water for 30 minutes and drained
65 gm / ½ cup	Almonds *(badam)*, blanched, peeled and sliced
400 gm	Condensed milk

METHOD

◆ Bring the milk to a boil with the cardamoms and add the rice. Cook, stirring regularly, until the milk is fully absorbed and the rice is tender and broken.
◆ Add the sultanas and the condensed milk. Cook, stirring regularly until the consistency is thick, and the *kheer* sticks to the ladle. Garnish with the almonds. Refrigerate and serve when cool.

DESSERTS

SHAHI TUKRA

(Rich bread dessert sprinkled with dry fruit)

Serves: 4

INGREDIENTS

4 slices	White bread cut into half, with the crust removed, shaped in triangles
10 ml / 2 tsp	Clarified butter *(ghee)* / refined oil
300 ml / 1½ cups	Milk, full cream
50 gm / 4 tbsp	Sugar
½ gm / ½ tsp	Saffron *(kesar)*, dissolved in 2 tbsp of hot water
8 gm / 10	Almonds *(badam)*, blanched, peeled and sliced
6 gm / 10	Sultanas *(kishmish)*, soaked in hot water for 15 minutes

METHOD

◆ Heat the oil and fry the bread triangles till golden in colour. Remove and drain on absorbent paper. Keep aside.
◆ Heat the clarified butter / oil in a large frying pan. Add the fried bread slices, pour the milk over them and sprinkle the sugar. Turn the slices over carefully to coat well and cook till the milk thickens and changes colour, stirring slowly all the time. Add the dissolved saffron. Sprinkle the almonds and sultanas.
◆ Turn the slices over, taking care that they do not break.

Shahi Tukra ▶

DESSERTS

SHRIKHAND

(Creamy, chilled yoghurt cheese)

Serves: 6-8

INGREDIENTS

1400 ml / 7 cups	Yoghurt *(dahi)*, hung in a muslin cloth for 2-3 hours to remove the moisture
	Castor sugar (for every cup of drained yoghurt, add 1 cup of castor sugar)
½ gm / ½ tsp	Saffron *(kesar)*, ground with 1 tbsp vetivier *(kewra)* essence
12	Green cardamoms *(elaichi)*, powdered
16 gm / 20	Almonds *(badam)*, blanched, peeled and sliced

METHOD

◆ In a serving bowl, mix the castor sugar into the yoghurt. Add the ground saffron, vetivier essence and the cardamom powder. Beat well. Add half the almonds and keep the rest for garnishing.
◆ Cover the bowl with a cling film and chill in a refrigerator for at least 1 hour. The *shrikhand* should have the consistency of thick cream. Remove the film and garnish with the remaining sliced almonds.

DAHI KA MEETHA

(Baked yoghurt with almonds and raisins)

Serves: 4-6

INGREDIENTS

1 lt	Milk
50 gm / ¼ cup	Sugar
1 gm / ½ tsp	Cardamom seed *(elaichi)* powder
10 gm / 12	Almonds *(badam)*, blanched, peeled and sliced
5 gm / 12	Sultanas *(kishmish)*, soaked in warm water for 15 minutes, drained
200 ml / 1 cup	Yoghurt *(dahi)*

METHOD

◆ Bring milk to a rapid boil; lower the heat and simmer, stirring continuously, until the milk is reduced to half the original quantity. Add the sugar, cardamom powder, almonds and sultanas. Mix well and keep aside to cool.
◆ Whisk the yoghurt until smooth. Stir it into the milk. Mix well. Pour this mixture into an oven-proof shallow dish. Bake in a moderately hot oven for 30 minutes or until it hardens. Refrigerate until chilled.

KAJU KE LADDU

(Cashewnut balls)

Serves: 4

INGREDIENTS

1 cup approx. / 110 gm	Cashewnuts *(kaju)*, roasted, ground to a crumbly powder
¾ cup approx. / 125 ml	Cold water
¼ cup approx. / 225 gm	Sugar
15 ml / 1 tbsp	Condensed milk
2 gm / 1 tsp	Green cardamom seed *(elaichi)* powder
15 gm / 1 tbsp	Sultanas *(kishmish)*, sliced
30 gm / 2 tbsp	Almonds *(badam)*, blanched, peeled and sliced

METHOD

◆ Boil the water with the sugar until a thick syrup is obtained. Add the condensed milk, cardamom powder and sultanas. Add ¾ of the ground cashewnuts and stir to make a thick paste.
◆ Pour the thick paste into a tray to cool. When cool, make small balls each, about the size of a golf ball, and roll the balls in the remaining cashewnut powder, coating them all over. Keep aside. Decorate with the sliced almonds.

138

Kaju Ke Laddu ▶

MEWA KA ZARDA

(Rice pudding enriched with condiments and dry fruit)

Serves: 4-6

INGREDIENTS

400 gm / 2 cups	Basmati rice, picked, washed, soaked in water for 1 hour and drained
200 ml / 1 cup	Refined oil
800 ml / 4 cups	Milk
3 gm / 1 ½ tsp	Green cardamom seed *(elaichi)* powder
½ gm / ¼ tsp	Nutmeg *(jaiphal)* powder
½ gm / ¼ tsp	Mace *(javitri)* powder
½ gm / ½ tsp	Saffron *(kesar)*, soaked in 2 tbsp hot milk
50 gm approx./½ cup	Charoli seeds *(chironji)*, coarsely ground
16 gm / 20	Almonds *(badam)*, blanched, peeled and sliced
25 gm / 20	Cashewnuts *(kaju)*, sliced
30 gm / ¼ cup	Sultanas *(kishmish)*, soaked in water for 15 minutes, drained
475 gm / 2 ½ cups	Sugar

METHOD

◆ Heat the oil in a deep pan; when hot, add the drained rice. Stir and add the milk. Stir to mix well. Cover the rice until it is cooked and the milk is fully absorbed.
◆ Add the cardamom, nutmeg and mace powders with the saffron milk, charoli seeds, almonds, cashewnuts, sultanas and sugar. Mix well.
◆ Cover the pan with a tight lid and put in an oven preheated to 100⁰ C / 212⁰ F. Bake for 10 to 12 minutes.

DESSERTS

BHINDI RAITA

(Fried okra in smooth yoghurt)

Serves: 4

INGREDIENTS

500 gm	Okra *(bhindi)*
	Refined oil for frying
400 ml / 2 cups	Yoghurt *(dahi)*
8 gm / 2 tbsp	Coriander leaves *(hara dhaniya)*, chopped
6 gm / 2	Green chillies *(hari mirch)*, chopped
1 ½ gm / 1 tsp	Red chilli *(lal mirch)* powder
3 gm / 1 tsp	Cumin seed *(jeera)* powder
	Salt to taste

METHOD

◆ Heat the oil in a wok *(kadhai)*; when hot, add the chopped okra. Fry stirring occasionally until crisp. Remove with a slotted spoon onto a absorbent paper. Keep aside.
◆ Whisk the yoghurt in a serving bowl with the coriander leaves, green chillies, fried okra and salt. Sprinkle with red chilli powder and cumin seed powder. Chill and serve.

ALU~ANANAS RAITA

(Potato-pineapple in yoghurt)

Serves: 4

INGREDIENTS

600 ml / 3 cups	Yoghurt *(dahi)*
1 cup	Pineapple cubes *(ananas)*, drained
1 cup	Potato cubes *(alu)*, boiled and skinned
1½ gm / 1 tsp	Red chilli *(lal mirch)* powder
3 gm / 1 tsp	Cumin seed *(jeera)* powder, roasted
	Salt to taste

METHOD

◆ Whisk the yoghurt in a serving bowl. Add the pineapple cubes, potato cubes and salt. Stir carefully, mixing well. Sprinkle with red chilli powder and roasted cumin seed powder. Chill and serve.

BOONDI RAITA

(Deep-fried chick pea flour pearls in creamy yoghurt)

Serves: 4

INGREDIENTS

600 ml / 3 cup	Yoghurt *(dahi)*
1 cup	Boondi
9 gm / 2 tbsp	Cumin seed *(jeera)*, roasted
2½ gm / 1½ tsp	Red chilli *(lal mirch)* powder
	Salt to taste

METHOD

◆ Whisk the yoghurt in a serving bowl, add all the ingredients and mix well. Chill and serve.

DHANIYA~PUDINA RAITA

(Fresh coriander-mint in chilled yoghurt)

Serves: 4

INGREDIENTS

Blend to form a smooth paste with 3 tbsp of water:

25 gm / 1 cup	Coriander leaves *(hara dhaniya)*, chopped
15 gm / 1 cup	Mint leaves *(pudina)*, chopped
12 gm / 4	Green chillies *(hari mirch)*, chopped
500 ml / 2½ cups	Yoghurt *(dahi)*
3 gm / 1 tsp	Cumin seed *(jeera)* powder
48 gm / 2 tbsp	Ginger *(adrak)*, chopped finely
	Salt to taste

METHOD

◆ Whisk the yoghurt in a serving bowl with the coriander and mint leaves and green chilli paste. Add the cumin seed powder, chopped ginger and salt. Mix well. Chill and serve.

Clockwise from top left: Bhindi Raita, Boondi Raita, ▶
Alu-Ananas Raita, Dhaniya-Pudina Raita

140

RAITAS

TAMATAR CHUTNEY

(Tomato chutney)

INGREDIENTS

30 ml / 2 tbsp	Mustard oil (sarson ka tel)
3 gm / 1 tsp	Mustard seeds (sarson)
5	Red chillies, whole, dry
2 cups	Tomatoes, skinned and chopped
½ cup	Brown sugar
60 gm / ½ cup	Sultanas (kishmish), soaked in water for 15 minutes and drained
2 tsp	Salt

METHOD

◆ Heat the mustard oil until it smokes. Remove the pan from the heat and cool. Replace the pan on medium heat and add the mustard seeds, dry red chillies and fry until the colour of the chillies changes. Add the chopped tomatoes. Mix well. Cover the pan and cook well; make a tomato paste. Add the brown sugar, sultanas and salt. Mix well and stir till sugar dissolves completely. The chutney should have a smooth, sauce-like consistency.

TIL~KHUS KHUS KI CHUTNEY

(Sesame-poppy seed chutney)

INGREDIENTS

Dry roast separately:

12 gm / 2 tbsp	Poppy (khus khus) seeds
18 gm / 2 tbsp	Sesame (til) seeds
2 gm / 1 tsp	Cumin (jeera) seeds
40 ml / 2½ tbsp	Refined oil
3 gm / 2 tsp	Red chilli (lal mirch) powder
9 gm / 2 tsp	Salt
½ cup	Tamarind (imli) extract
3½ gm / 1 tsp	Brown sugar
200 ml / 1 cup	Water

METHOD

◆ Heat the oil in a saucepan; add the roasted seeds and other ingredients. Cook, stirring occasionally until ¾ of the water has evaporated. Remove the pan from the heat and cool.
◆ When cool, blend to make a chutney with a sauce-like consistency.

NARIYAL CHUTNEY

(Coconut chutney)

INGREDIENTS

30 ml / 2 tbsp	Refined oil
3 gm / 1 tsp	Mustard seeds (sarson)
10	Curry leaves (meethi neem ke patte)

15 gm / 5	Green chillies (hari mirch), chopped
1 tbsp	Black gram (urad dal), husked, split
120 gm / ½	Coconut (nariyal), grated
12 gm / 2 tbsp	Tamarind (imli) extract, Salt to taste

METHOD

◆ Heat the oil in a shallow pan. Reduce heat and add all the ingredients except the taramind. Stir well. Add the tamarind extract. Cook until most of the water evaporates.
◆ When cool, blend to make a smooth paste.

DHANIYA~PUDINA CHUTNEY

(Coriander-mint chutney)

INGREDIENTS

25 gm / 1 cup	Coriander leaves (hara dhaniya)
15 gm / 1 cup	Mint leaves (pudina)
½ cup	Curry leaves (meethi neem ke patte)
60 gm / ½ cup	Garlic (lasan) powder
¼ cup	Green chillies (hari mirch)
3 gm / 2 tsp	Cumin (jeera) seeds
95 gm / ½ cup	Sugar
100 ml / ½ cup	Tamarind (imli) extract
9 gm / 2 tsp	Salt

METHOD

◆ Blend all the ingredients with 2-3 tbsp of water into a chutney with a sauce-like consistency.

SONTH

(Dried ginger powder chutney)

INGREDIENTS

1 cup	Tomato (tamatar) purée
60 gm / ½ cup	Sultanas (kishmish), soaked in water for 15 minutes
100 gm / ½ cup	Jaggery (gur), diluted in ¾ cup hot water
2 gm / ½ tsp	Dry ginger powder (sonth)
1½ gm / 1 tsp	Fennel seed (saunf), powder
100 ml / ½ cup	Tamarind (imli) extract
30 ml / 2 tbsp	Refined oil, Salt to taste

METHOD

◆ Heat the oil. Reduce heat to medium; add all the ingredients. Stir well. Reduce heat further; cook until the oil rises and the chutney has a sauce-like consistency.

Top: Tamatar Chutney, Til-Khus Khus Ki Chutney ▶
Centre: Nariyal Chutney
Bottom: Dhaniya-Pudina Chutney, Sonth

INDEX

INDEX